PRAISE FOR *SEVEN STEPS*

"*Wise and inspiring, this is a wonderful book for anyone wanting to deepen their relationship with the angelic realm.*" William Bloom, spiritual teacher, founder of the Spiritual Companions Trust, co-founder of the Alternatives Programme, London, and author of *Working with Angels*, among other titles

"*A completely practical guide to harnessing the power of the angels in your everyday life. Anyone wanting to learn more about working with angels will be wisely and lovingly guided by this book.*" Deb Hawken, author of *Who am I, Where am I, What is this Place?*

"*In this book Chrissie has achieved the almost impossible task of translating her face-to-face charisma and 'presence' into the written word. If you can't get onto a course with Chrissie herself, this book is the next best thing.*" Dr Carl Stonier PhD, psychotherapist, Energy Psychology practitioner

"*I absolutely love this book, not only for its wealth of angelic information, but because the angels have showered their radiance through every word.*" Dianne Pegler, author of *The Sacred Order of the Magi*

"*Chrissie's knowledge of, and connection with, the angels is evident from the very start. If anyone doubts their own ability to connect with angels, and wishes to 'sway to the music of the stars', this is the book to read.*" Barbara Meiklejohn-Free, author of *The Highland Seer*

"*We are all looking for a bright star to help us on the path of spiritual ennobling, and, in a constellation of many stars, some can be beguiling but disappointing. Yet here is a star, in the form of this book, that elevates and shines with purity, wisdom and purpose.*" Stewart Pearce, Master of Voice, Angel Whisperer, Voice Alchemist and Author

"*Chrissie Astell's work is a continuing inspiration for those who tread the spiritual path. Grounded in a practical approach, it is over-lighted by powerful and positive angelic energies that keep it securely within a deeply heart-based pattern of loving service.*" Stuart Wilson, co-author of *The Essenes: Children of the Light* and author of *Beyond Limitations: The Power of Conscious Co-Creation*

SEVEN STEPS INTO ANGEL LIGHT

A JOURNEY OF SELF-DISCOVERY AND SPIRITUAL EMPOWERMENT

CHRISSIE ASTELL

WATKINS

Sharing Wisdom Since 1893

For my grandchildren,
Daniel, Sofia, Nicolas, Olivia, Melody, Josefina
Six beautiful souls on their own magical journey
With all my love

This edition first published in the UK and USA 2017 by
Watkins, an imprint of Watkins Media Limited
19 Cecil Court
London WC2N 4EZ

enquiries@watkinspublishing.com

Design and typography copyright © Watkins Media Limited 2017
Text copyright © Chrissie Astell 2017

10 9 8 7 6 5 4 3 2 1

Designed and typeset by JCS Publishing Services Ltd
Printed and bound by CPI Group (UK) Ltd, Croydon, CR0 4YY
A CIP record for this book is available from the British Library
ISBN: 978-1-78678-058-4

www.watkinspublishing.com

CONTENTS

ACKNOWLEDGEMENTS

It's actually quite difficult to write an acknowledgement of all the help I've received in putting this latest book together. There are so many people who have influenced my life path, my "career" over the last two decades that I find it quite emotional to remember all the wonderful events, workshops, training sessions, meetings and gatherings that have enabled and empowered me. And so I must thank everyone and anyone who has helped me in organizing, supporting and being present in exactly the right way at the right time to help me step up and shine my Light. They are all angels!

First, I'd like to thank all the wonderful real-life teachers who have played a part in the enlightening process of my own particular journey towards the Light. All the authors that nudged my awakening, the therapist who enabled me to discover my inner strength many years ago, and all the loving friends and fellow travellers along the way. Some journeyed far along the path and have now gone, others stayed for a short while and taught me great lessons, and others are still with me. I'm so grateful for all their support and encouragement.

I'd like to thank all my Essene family, especially Anne MacEwen and Jackie Stevenson who had the belief and confidence in me to ordain me as celebrant – it has been such a blessing and taught me so much on many levels.

To Patricia Masson, Iren Dibble and Josie Remzi, my friends and honest sounding boards. Thank you.

Thanks, too, to the "Surrey, SDF group", Sarah Rozenthuler, Anita Hughes, Peter Danby, Andrew Woodgate and Christopher Frampton – you have been and still are inspiring friends, thank you all, just for being there.

Thanks too to William Bloom and all my Spiritual Companions Trust Educator colleagues and friends for including me in their amazing achievements.

In acknowledging and thanking supportive friends I must include all the lovely folk in Ireland (north and south) who've continually supported my work (so many – you know who you are) and David Lister and Juliet Green in West Crete, who have given me the opportunity to spread my wings and take my work overseas.

I'd like to thank Kelly Thompson and Jo Lal at Watkins, for encouraging me and giving me the opportunity to adapt my "Educating Heart and Soul" course into *Seven Steps into Angel Light*, and Vicky Hartley and Jillian Levick and the marketing/publicity team for their talents and tenacity to "get it out there". To my editor Sandy Draper: you are amazing, thank you for all your hard work.

Big, big thanks go to Richard Haywood, my business partner, for all his organization, practical and technical support, for tolerating my inefficiency and remaining a good friend, and his wife Helen. The lovely Maggie Stewart, who has also become a dear friend, without whom my workshops would not be the same.

With a heart full of love and gratitude I thank my own family, and my long-suffering husband Brian for his tolerance and understanding. I am away so much of the time! My mother Sylvia Moss and father Fred Astell, whose distant love was always with me, and whose genetic mystical mantle I clearly took up. My sister Stella, and Mary, for their love and positive input, to my son Dan for proving that flying high is always possible, and daughter Claire, whose faith shines through adversity and who is a constant source of loving inspiration and mutual support. Then, thank you to all my gorgeous little angels, my grandchildren, whose unconditional loving hearts and faces light up my life like the stars in the sky.

And finally, my gratitude – immeasurable – to my angelic helpers, and the universal consciousness I know as God, to the pure Light, who, for me, is always, always there throughout.

Thank you. Thank you. Thank you.

FOREWORD

In *Seven Steps into Angel Light*, Chrissie Astell presents a comprehensive programme for developing your relationship with the angels. She puts the phenomenon of the human connection with the angelic realm into a broad spiritual context, and provides many recipes for making that connection conscious. As with all good recipes, these leave room for you to adjust them to your own personal taste.

You should understand, however, that your personal taste will evolve in the process of any adjustment you make. The seven Archangels that the book calls are no mere references on a page. They are mighty energies. Those energies inform the book and they will inform you even as you read. Should you invite them to connect with you more consciously, they will do so in ways that will sometimes astound you.

If you're a beginner with this kind of work, *Seven Steps into Angel Light* will guide you gently as you open up your awareness of yourself and develop a wider spiritual perspective. If you have already become aware of your essential spiritual nature and you're looking to anchor more deeply into it, this book will provide you with exercises to assist you with that objective.

As you deepen your connection, it's natural if some of your experiences become intense. The author recognizes that healing the residual effects of old wounds to your energetic constitution cannot be put off. She makes it clear that it's not always easy to "... bring love back into our life and begin the challenging process of forgiveness and reconciliation". The value of trusting the Archangels to support you with this is simply inestimable.

Seven Steps into Angel Light is the work of someone who has dedicated her life to exploring the angelic connection. Chrissie has committed to this connection and embodied it as a service to the awakening in human consciousness. In this book she shares her wisdom and experience in practical and accessible ways.

The angels will become your teachers if you engage with the processes given in this book. They will, as Chrissie says, "... help you expand your awareness of who you are". They will "help you follow your spiritual impulse and discover your soul purpose..."

Altazar Rossiter PhD
Author of *Developing Spiritual Intelligence*

INTRODUCTION

STEP INTO DIVINE LIGHT
WITHIN AND WITHOUT

"When you are inspired by some great purpose, some extraordinary project, all your thoughts break their bonds: Your mind transcends limitations, your consciousness expands in every direction, and you find yourself in a new, great and wonderful world."

The Yoga Sutras of Patanjali

We live in a world where communication is instantaneous, where it is possible to travel from one side of the planet to the other in less than a day and we are able to access endless amounts of information with just the click of a button. However, in spite of, or perhaps because of, this insta-connected digital environment, we are also living in a world in which many people feel more disconnected than ever before. And perhaps – having turned away from organized religion and the teachings of our upbringing because they no longer feel right – that is why more and more of us are searching for something "more". In fact, the original meaning of the Latin term *religare* ("religion") is "to reconnect" (*re-* meaning "again" and *-ligare* "to connect"), so whatever your faith or your cultural background, the overriding impulse that so many of us experience is to seek and reconnect with what can be called the "Divine Light".

I have felt it too: a yearning for something I couldn't name. Until I realized that it was the most natural desire of all: a spiritual impulse that guided me back to my innermost self, deep within my heart and soul. You may be a seeker too, searching for ways to reconnect, and my hope is that *Seven Steps into Angel Light* will give you the nudge you need to allow you to access a deeper level of fulfilment, to find what might be called your "soul purpose" by finally acknowledging that quiet voice inside you – the one that whispers: "Surely there is more to life than this?"

My own searching led me to follow my heart, where I found a passion for working with the powerful energy of angels. I call this energy "Angel Light". I hope that, as you step into this Light with me in the pages that follow, you will also discover and enhance your own "Light" – your inner and outer radiance. By engaging with your own personal spiritual impulse, you'll be able to live more authentically, more holistically and more purposefully, whether at work, at home or as part of a larger community.

Angels, as messengers and protectors, have been linked with humanity for centuries. They have played a role in every world religion since the Egyptians and were depicted in cave art even before that. Perhaps that is why so many of us are drawn to them. Even those who say they don't believe in angels will often admit to having experienced a presence or guiding spirit in their lives that they couldn't explain.

Often this intuitive connection to angels manifests as a result of a trauma or crisis that sends you spiralling downwards until you hit rock bottom. Sometimes it can be a life-changing mystical experience, like a vision, a near-death experience or a miraculous recovery, leaving you with a sense of having a deeper "purpose" to fulfil in life. Or perhaps you simply desire a more peaceful, more enlightened, more joyous way of being. Whatever your reason for picking up this book, whatever your faith (or lack thereof), welcome. The Light of the angels awaits you.

My spiritual quest for the Light

In my childhood there was plenty of room for fairies, magic, diversity and spirituality. My father was a mystic and a healer, and he and my mother took separate roads, both embarking on their own extraordinary spiritual quests. Fortunately, I was blessed to be raised by a grandma who believed in past lives, tea-leaf reading, palmistry and Jesus – who I was told wanted me for a "sunbeam". She was right of course! And this unorthodox upbringing gave me independence and confidence, which proved to be invaluable training for my later years.

It is hard to pinpoint when my work with angels really started because I have felt their presence throughout my life. Indeed, I have had so many encounters and mystical experiences that I filled a book (*Gifts from Angels*) with my and other people's wonderful angel stories. But even though I've always had faith in God and the Divine, it became obvious to me that I had been suppressing my spirituality for many years. I wasn't living my truth or being authentic.

Stepping up and learning how to live a more spiritually motivated existence was a massive turning point in my life. I had always pondered the really big questions, like why I was here, but in my early thirties my life was in turmoil. I felt I had a different, bigger role to play but, frustratingly, couldn't quite work out what it was. At that time, I didn't understand that I had created this dilemma by ignoring my heart and intuition. I was doing a job I hated and simultaneously struggling in an unhappy marriage. After 10 years of soul-searching, I realized that the only way to satisfy this yearning for something "more" was to end my marriage and head off in search of a deeper purpose. It was only then that I began to heed my heart, and this is when I began to feel compelled to work with the angelic realms.

After that, a series of literally life-changing encounters, mysterious synchronicities and coincidences enhanced my understanding. It started in 1997, when I was invited by my mother to attend a four-day retreat, organized by people who called themselves "New Essenes".[1] It was there that I learned a new way of communing with nature and angels. Each day led me deeper towards a spiritual practice, which I can only describe as "stepping up" into the Light of angels – in the sense that I discovered my own Higher Self: my personal Angel Light. It was from that point I was able to recognize my calling and respond.

My new life started to take shape from the moment I decided to trust my intuition and develop my abilities as a healer. One of my mystical angelic encounters drew me to an event where I noticed an artist who painted angels in exactly the same style as my mother. Upon discovering that the artist also taught "angelic healing", I quickly signed up for her courses and it was not long before we were working together. I also felt inspired by the angels to write and teach my own workshops. By this time I was single again and working as a nurse to support myself, so I was able to dedicate my life to my calling, going wherever I felt the Divine inspiration to follow. Coincidence and synchronicity led me to university, where I met wonderful people and many new interconnecting doors opened.

Even now, when some of the places I'm sent seem obscure, there is always a reason, whether my mission is to heal a place, just one person, or simply to carry the Light into a community. There is always personal learning, too. Wherever I'm sent, the angels have an agenda of love and service that I have a part in fulfilling.

Now, 20 years on, I have met hundreds of people in my workshops who also feel drawn by a similarly strong impulse to find deeper meaning in their lives. Whether they choose to tap into angelic guidance to help them find their purpose or not, they have all "woken up" and are conscious of their desire for a more fulfilling life that's inclusive of their path. And in my role as spiritual facilitator and teacher, it is in reconnecting people of all faiths and backgrounds with the "lightness" and wisdom of the angelic realms that brings me most pleasure. For me, angels are beings made of particles of light that have a purer, higher frequency or vibration than ours: a vast energetic expression of the mind of the Divine – God, Creator, Source, whatever word you prefer to use to describe the vast universal energy that was present in the creation of the Universe, our planet Earth and us.

This pure, loving Divine Angel Light is within and around us all, and it is available to everyone. By inviting the angelic forces of the brightest, purest love to come closer – and by understanding how we can communicate and work with these powerful energies – we literally raise our own vibration and enhance our life experience.

The great energy exchange

While the masters of "ancient wisdom" and our great spiritual leaders have acknowledged this transference of light (in the form of prayer and angelic communication) for thousands of years, scientists are only now starting to catch on, using quantum physics to validate such mystical teachings. Studies – especially in Germany, Austria and Switzerland – have shown how quantum particles of light are stored and released by our DNA on a daily basis.[2] This cellular light can be measured with specialist camera equipment and so illustrates the dynamic interplay of this web of light exchange surrounding everything. Violet light emitting from the cells indicates a higher vibration, but the vibration decreases as light particles are lost. Interestingly, if no light is emitted (in other words, light is held back for some reason), the same camera equipment shows that the process of reabsorption creates heat in the cell, which also lowers the energetic vibration.

In spiritual terms we see this phenomenon playing out in our lives, too. When we suppress our Light, or our true self, it disrupts us at a cellular level and lowers our energy vibration. This inevitably impacts how we feel, our health and overall wellbeing. I think most of us have experienced this lower energy vibration: we feel sluggish and not our vibrant selves. We also know we can transmit how we feel to others, when we cheer someone up with a smile, for example. So, even though our Light cannot usually be measured or seen by the naked eye, we know it exists.

All the evidence points to the fundamental nature of this exchange of light energy – to all of life's processes. And, if you think about it, even the concept of prayer as a light form is not as impossible as it might sound. Our Universe is made up entirely of particles containing that same light. We human beings are as intrinsic to the Universe as the mountains and the stars, and literally exchange information with it via light emitted and received through our cells. This means that thoughts, words, gestures and emotions emanate from our bodies as "light" energy too.

Just as you might have experienced the light of love beaming from another's eyes, without a word being spoken, so this energy can be sent into the Universe and picked up by the vast angelic beings as an instant transmission.

In this book you'll learn how to connect and communicate with seven of these beneficent angels of Light, known as Archangels, who will guide you in raising your own energetic vibration.

Throughout the ages there have been countless reports of angelic encounters. However, angels do not generally appear as physical, human-shaped entities as they are so often portrayed in art. Rather, angels tend to make their presence known to us through our highly sophisticated senses. Personally, I think of angels as vast swathes of vibrant, brilliant-coloured light that inhabit the Earth's atmosphere. And, while it seems almost bizarre nowadays to imagine heaven as an actual place somewhere above the clouds, where the Divine sits on a throne surrounded by angels, we do now know that there is certainly an invisible energetic "field".[3] I believe that in this "heavenly" place there is only love, light and peace. And it is here that these energy beings that we think of as angels reside.

FEMININE AND MASCULINE ENERGIES

The Bible and other historical scripts describe angels in masculine terms, but this portrayal changed in the Victorian era when kind, compassionate and charitable women were described as "angels". It is not gender, however, that gives us a sense of their masculinity or femininity, but the *quality* of a particular angel's energy. When you connect with an angel's essence, or are graced by a vision or visitation, you may certainly feel an extraordinary sense of either masculinity or femininity, but it is the subtle sense of the angel's energetic qualities, rather than their gender, that is important.

You too are a Being of Light having a human experience in a physical body. And it is in the blending of energy between your physical body and the presence of Angel Light that you will feel their Divine presence.

If an angel was to present itself in human form, or in sparkles of light or an orb, for example, what we would sense is only a tiny particle of the angel's essence. Not, as some would interpret, the entire being. An angel's Light would be too vast, too powerful, too bright and altogether far too much for us to take in. But once experienced (for whatever reason), the essence of that angel stays with us all the time, guiding us and surrounding us in love. These are our "guardian angels" – and all we have to do is learn how to become aware of their guidance.

The Seven Steps

In this book, you'll be working with the Light of seven Archangels. These angelic beings represent seven major types of light or divine qualities that could be said to make up the Universe. I've been working with the Divine influence of these angels since I was called to dedicate my life to this work. By combining work with the Seven Rays of Divinity in the study of Theosophy[4] and the associated seven Archangels, then learning about the beliefs and spiritual practices of the Essenes, I found my spiritual calling. I've written other books about the Archangels, including *Discovering Angels*, *Advice from Angels* and *Gifts from Angels,* plus my angel oracle card kits, but in this book I wanted to provide a different approach: a personal, guided journey to help you enhance your connection to the angelic realms and discover your own unique spiritual path. The following seven steps have not only proved immensely helpful in my own life but I also use them in my workshops and as part of my home study course, "Educating Heart and Soul".

> Learning how to raise your energetic vibration and tune into this heavenly light form is a bit like tuning in to a radio receiver: you may sense the presence of love, hear messages of reassurance and guidance or receive healing.

Each of the seven steps corresponds to a specific Archangel that will help guide you on your journey from awakening, or calling, through personal discovery towards greater spiritual development. Each Archangel has a colour, a vibrational resonance and an immeasurable, powerful energy of love, which was described as a "flame" by the Theosophical Society. Theosophists related these light vibrations into what is called the "Seven Rays" or "flames" – divisions, or emanations of light from the Absolute Light of the Divine. Each corresponds to a day of the week, a colour of the spectrum and an aspect of human nature.

It is hard to imagine the sheer size of these Divine energies, as they spread across our Universe like layers of a gigantic rainbow. They are everywhere and, when called upon, can manifest in a form that we can perhaps see or feel as a presence, a Being of Light.

Every step in the pages that follow builds on the one before. You might like to think of the process as similar to ascending a flight of stairs in a high-rise building, where each floor represents one stage of the journey. The ground floor is where we begin, and then we progress to the higher floors. We have the option to stay on one floor for a while, or pop down to revisit any of the floors we have passed earlier. Each stage is a building block, adding further dimensions to what you have already learned, and throughout the journey is a strong current of love that will, I trust, help to lift your wings. Spiritual practice can be arduous, but it can also be a real joy. You may take each stage as ardently or "lightly" as you wish.

I am not promising that at the end of the Seven Steps you will reach the lofty heights of Nirvana – a dawning of fulfillment or total spiritual ascension. But I have faith that the journey itself will simultaneously quench your thirst for greater understanding of self while whetting your appetite for even more knowledge. It will also bring greater wisdom and stronger connections with the Divine energies of the angelic realms.

Our aim in setting off on this journey is to raise our vibration and turn up the Light within.

WHY SEVEN STEPS?

In Numerology (the study of the hidden significance of numbers), seven is sacred and holds the energy of the "ancient mystics".[5] The number seven is very important in many legends and ancient myths too, as well as religious texts, including the Qur'an, the Torah and the Bible. In the Old Testament, for example, we are told that the world was created in seven days. In Zoroastrianism, the Great Lord of the Light brought in six other divine aspects of himself to assist with creation. In Judaism, the people of Israel mourned for seven days and in Egypt the number seven symbolizes eternal life. In Buddhism, the sacred lotus flower of Buddha's pedestal has seven main petals, and in yoga there are seven major chakras (see Tools for Your Journey, page 27). The number seven also has connections with Greece, Babylon, Iran (Persia) and numerous other ancient civilizations, including the texts of the Hindu *Rigveda*, which is considered the oldest written book on the planet (c.1,500–1,200 BCE).

The Seven Steps will help and inspire you to:

- Develop deeper self-knowledge and wisdom.
- Experience enhanced creativity.
- Develop your "higher" and more fulfilling life purpose.
- Open up to attract and share pure, unconditional love.
- Learn and use techniques for protection and grounding.
- Transmute negative feelings into positive energy.
- Recognize, honour and respect all individual journeys.

- Feel an increased sense of inner peace and wellbeing.
- Encourage others to open their hearts to forgiveness and healing.
- Use angelic healing energies to raise consciousness.
- Gain an understanding of different types of mystical and religious beliefs.

In so doing, the Seven Steps form an intuitive map that you can use to find the direction of your spiritual journey, by enabling you to reflect upon, revise, reassess or re-educate your thoughts – and so open a door to a new perspective or a re-remembering of forgotten wisdom that will enrich and revitalize your life.

The truth is that you have never lost your connection to the angels or their Light, so as you reconnect to the unique vibration of the Divine spark of Light, you will also rediscover the powerful Divinity within your self – the part of you that is brought alive and filled with awe and delight, wonder and amazement at the sheer beauty and magnificence of our beautiful world, which some people call their soul.

This is the purpose of *Seven Steps into Angel Light* – to help you use this magic to expand your awareness of who you are. To help you follow your spiritual impulse, discover your soul purpose and live a more fulfilled, connected, contented life.

TOOLS FOR YOUR JOURNEY

HOW TO GET THE BEST FROM THIS BOOK

"We delight in the beauty of the butterfly, but rarely admit the changes it has gone through to achieve that beauty."

Maya Angelou

Before starting to work with the energy of the angels, it is important to take a few moments to reflect upon your intentions for the journey ahead. Often we only use prayer, contemplation or meditation to call upon angels (or the Divine of whatever denomination or creed) when we are desperate, or in despair. But one of the spiritual Laws of the Universe, taught by all great teachers throughout time, is "ask and you shall receive". So, provided you seek with a pure heart for the best possible outcome, then your prayers will always be heard and answered. What is more, the angels rejoice at the reawakening of a friend as, with practice, your Light shines ever brighter. I like to imagine it's almost as if a beacon or flare is ignited from the top of your head that says, "Here I am!" or, "I'm back!" The fact is that we are *all* loved, and the angels have always been on hand, waiting for you to make a choice to return to the highest calling of your soul.

> Angels are bounteous, beneficent, beautiful beings of pure Light who act only on the will of the Divine and resonate with the vibration of complete and absolute Divine love.

As I said before, it is best to call in the Angel Light with an open heart, with gratitude and with the "best and highest possible outcome for all concerned" in mind. At the end of your communication – whether it is for the purposes of healing, guidance, inner peace or to simply make a connection – always remember to express your thanks to the Universe, the Divine, the angels and the Light within you too.

A WORD OF WARNING

All requests, whether positive or negative, selfless or self-centred, are heard by the angels – and your prayers will always be answered – but the outcome may not always be as you expect. So be careful not to request anything that may be harmful to anyone else. An angel cannot change your "karma"[1] – only you can do that, by working on behaviour patterns that need changing. Remember: be careful what you wish for!

Following the Seven Steps

The Seven Steps reflect my own understanding of the seven Archangels and how these seven beneficent Light Beings can help us connect with seven different human attributes and levels of spiritual energy. These are my guiding steps to set out on a path of personal and spiritual exploration:

Step 1: Connect to Archangel Gabriel, the great "Annunciator", the message-bringer, instigator of new projects and new beginnings. Working with Gabriel's brilliant white Light will help strengthen your communication with both your Higher Self and your angelic helpers. The practical exercises will teach you how to communicate with the angels, notice signs and reflect on your journey so far.

Step 2: Step into Archangel Jophiel's great yellow Light to discover great wisdom and creativity. During this step you may experience many "light-bulb" moments of recognition as you begin to see how we co-create our world. The practical exercises will help you to explore and "feel into" your spiritual impulse; you'll start to recognize the signs that point to your calling in life: your soul's purpose.

Step 3: Learn to call upon the protective "sword and armour" of the great Archangel Michael whenever spiritual strength and fortitude are required. You will find that his powerful blue Light becomes a grounding force on your journey. This step also shows you how to protect your aura and explores the spiritual and practical aspects of discernment. The practical exercises will show you how to cut the ties that bind you to memories and behaviours that no longer serve you and block your spiritual growth, your material success and your ability to live by your own "truth".

Step 4: Step into Archangel Raphael's balancing green Light to help you focus your energies on healing, so that you can fully release the past and ready yourself to step into the life that you want. The practical exercises take a deeper look at "body-talk", helping you recognize emotional toxins at a cellular level, as well as showing you how to release, cleanse and heal them.

Step 5: Feel the embrace of Archangel Chamuel's pink Light and let go of harmful thoughts that have prevented you from loving yourself and others in the past. By exploring the great spiritual teachings you will gain a deeper understanding of the Golden Thread of truth and love that intertwines the roots of all our world religions. The practical exercises explore ways of increasing self-esteem, developing a sense of self-love and attracting meaningful relationships into your life.

Step 6: Let go of any negative behaviour patterns and embrace the gift of transformation, joy and freedom with Archangel Zadkiel, the guardian of a powerful transform-ational Light: the Violet Flame. The practical exercises will ask you to reflect upon any negative energy that you may be holding onto (often subconsciously) and allow the angels to transmute it into positive energy, to free you from any harsh self-judgement and bring renewed joy and passion into your everyday experience.

Step 7: Tune into how you can be of service to others, within your community and to the planet, with Archangel Uriel, the guardian of the Earth. Working with Uriel's gold and ruby Light you will also discover how to create more peace as you move onwards in your journey. The practical exercises will help you to focus your energies on putting love into action and serving "the highest good" in everything you do.

Working through the book step by step

As I mentioned above, each step of the journey is supported with practices: reflections, self-enquiry exercises and guided meditations, as well as prayers and affirmations. So, no matter how busy your schedule, you can explore the ideas in your own time. However, to get the most from the Seven Steps, I'd suggest that you allow plenty of time for the practical work and use a journal for your thoughts and reflections along the way. At the end of each step, you might like to take note of your answers to the following questions:

- Do I fully understand this?
- How does this sit with my faith or set of beliefs?
- What lessons can I learn from this step?
- What practical guidance can I take from this that may be useful now in my life?

Angel associations

Before setting out on each step, take note of the "Angel Associations" panel. You may like to use the associated colour(s), planet(s), crystal(s), day of the week, element and ashram (a centre of heightened spiritual energy, see also page 30) to help you connect more deeply with the Archangel during your practical work.

For example, you might say prayers that connect to a particular Archangel on a particular day of the week, or add the appropriate crystal to your sacred space (see page 23, below) or light an appropriately coloured candle before starting one of the practices. Alternatively, you might choose to work with the Archangel's particular element by meditating outdoors in the fresh air or near water, for example.

Guided meditations

Some of the exercises have been created into sheets for you to print off and use. There are also meditative visualizations (called "guided meditations"), similar to the written ones, accompanying each step. These are designed to help you step into Angel Light, and can also be downloaded from the website: www.AngelLight.co.uk/sevensteps. There are no

17

rules for how often you use these practices, so please feel free to use any of them at any time. You may find that a particular Archangel meditation calls to you more often and becomes your favourite – that is fine.

Meditation has many physical and mental health benefits for the body and mind. These include reducing blood pressure and heart rate, clearing and calming the mind, reducing stress and suppressing appetite.[2-3] On a spiritual level, meditation has a balancing effect on the body, mind and soul. With practice, meditation can help you to become more aware and conscious of your thoughts, actions and beliefs, allowing you to experience a deeper connection with your own environment, the natural world and its elements and the Divine – whatever that means for you.

Preparing for meditation can be as simple as dedicating a little time each day, perhaps just after waking up, before eating breakfast, to focus your thoughts and still your body. It doesn't require any special equipment (unless you want it to). Simply find a place where you will be undisturbed, turn off your phone and focus on your breath for as long you wish to.

CREATING A MEDITATION PRACTICE

You many like to personalize your meditation. For example, by lighting a candle before you start, burning some aromatherapy oils or incense, and/or playing some soothing music (see also "Angel Associations"). To connect with one of the Archangels during your practice, simply call their name three times. (The number three has powerful mystical properties that magnify the intention of your prayer or request and has been used for thousands of years in spiritual rituals.) Whether you enjoy a more ritualistic approach or not, it is important to develop a safe space for your practice (see page 23) and to make sure that you are completely comfortable.

Some people like to sit cross-legged on the floor; others prefer to lie down with their knees supported or to sit in an upright chair with cushions to support their back. It is always best to have your spine as straight as possible with your head supported, and some teachers insist on sitting in an upright position so that all the energy centres, known as chakras (see page 27), are in alignment, with the crown facing upwards to connect with the Divine energies. Choose what feels right for you each time, but try not to fall asleep. That may be relaxing, but it isn't meditation.

PRACTICE 1
Becoming more aware of your breath

The simplest meditation practice is breath awareness. The aim of this is to allow your mind to be at peace by simply observing your breathing. Any form of meditation takes practice, so if you're new to it, start by practising for just 2–10 minutes a day and then build up your meditation muscle until you can sit comfortably for 20–30 minutes, then an hour or longer. Even a few minutes each day has a measurably positive effect.

1. Start by closing your eyes and taking a few deep breaths to release any tension from your body.
2. Then simply breathe in and out, observing the sensation as the air passes in through your nostrils, down through your body and out again.
3. If you notice your mind starting to wander, acknowledge the thought and bring your focus back to your breath.
4. If you find it helpful, say the following lines while observing the flow of breath: "Breathing in I am filled with energy and light. Breathing out I am relaxed and calm."

Once you have mastered the art of breathing deeply, it is best to let go of the words and simply breathe calmly.

Other types of meditation practices include walking, yoga and tai-chi, as well as many different types of guided visualization, such as shamanic journeying.

Some of the guided meditations in this book include note-taking. This might seem strange at first but simply follow the instructions and breathe calmly into a relaxed state while holding your pen and paper, ready to record any messages or insights you receive. These can then be interpreted later.

You may receive messages in the form of visions, symbols, colours, sensations or images during your meditation. Just make a note of them, withholding judgement or analysis for the moment, and accept each one with gratitude as a symbolic gift from the angels, the Divine, your guides[4] or Higher Self. What might not seem to make sense at first may become clearer as you progress through the Seven Steps.

JOURNAL THE SEVEN STEPS

Keep your journal and pen nearby while reading and before using any of the practices, so you can make notes and record your answers to the reflection and self-enquiry questions and exercises.

Affirmations

Throughout the book you'll find affirmations to support your journey and help you to reconnect to Angel Light. Affirmations are positive sentences that you repeat as often as you like in order to shift from negative self-belief to positive, and they are one of the most powerful tools for change. Everything we think and every word we utter is an affirmation. The power and energy created by the thought and then transmitted into sound through the word spoken is heard again through our senses, and as we hear it we believe it. This is why it is so important to be consciously aware of the tone and words we use. It is always possible to catch what we say, especially if it is negative, and make a point to change it into something positive.

For example, if you experience a lack of money but say, "Oh I am always so broke, I cannot afford to do the things I want", then you'll likely find that this situation doesn't change. If, however, you say, "I'm getting better at looking after my money", you'll find you will improve. And if you say, "I'm brilliant with money; the more I have the more it multiplies. I can afford everything I'd like to do", then you can start to break down the blockages preventing you from attracting financial abundance. This is the Law of Attraction.[5]

There's nothing New Age about affirmations. Although my intention throughout this book is to be non-denominational and all encompassing, some of the mainstream religious texts are very useful when it comes to illustrating the ancient wisdom. Affirmations, for example, are found in the Old Testament. In the book of Joel, from around 800 BCE, we can find the instruction: "Let the weak man say 'I Am strong.'" (Joel 3.10 NIV) When Moses encountered the burning bush and was greeted by the voice of God, he was told that the name of God was "I AM that I AM", meaning the Divinity within everything. "I AM in everything in creation. The light in all things." When we use the words "I AM", we are in fact connecting to the Divine presence deep within us all – the God/Goddess Within, the Divine Light, which we call the "I AM Presence". So use "I AM" to acknowledge the Light within you.

Daily prayers

At the end of each step, you will find a prayer for deepening your connection to that particular Archangel. These have been added to support you and you can use them as often or as little as you like. Some people love using prayer as a ritual at the start and the end of each day. For others – especially those who are not particularly religious – prayer can be thought of as sending a message to a friend, just to say, "Hi, I'm here and thinking about you." All gratitude and guidance prayers are sent into the light and received. They keep the lines of communication open.

Of course, if you have a favourite, then just use that one. If you find some of the words more appealing than others, feel free to edit or use as a basis to write your own. Everything in this book is for you to make your own, so use whatever works best for you.

Creating sacred space for the practices

Before setting out on the Seven Steps, you might like to dedicate a small area in your home for quiet reflection, meditation and other practical work. All faiths and cultures since the birth of humanity have created "sacred spaces". They can be found in natural landscapes, such as rock formations, mountaintops, waterfalls and even hawthorn bushes, or built on consecrated land. Wherever it is, whether we are conducting rituals, meditating for world peace or connecting with angels, we need a safe and sacred space for our work.

It is in these sacred and often very beautiful places where we may first connect on a deep and profound level with the great universal forces of the spiritual world. It is in these places where often we feel the presence of others, either human or angelic, hear voices or music, experience physical sensations, or see clear visions. Even if none of these experiences apply to you, you may have simply felt a sense of deep calm when standing at the top of a mountain, in a forest, by a lake or stone circle, or sitting quietly in an old church or beautiful temple.

Angels bring joy and healing but their power can be overwhelming, so calling them in to help create your space, if you want to, shouldn't be done flippantly. Although you can call upon any of the angels, including your guardian angel, spirit guides and ancestors, for assistance, it is Archangel Raphael (the Angel of Consecration) whose role it is to help you create a truly sacred space.

You may like to use crystals and light a candle or some essential oils in a burner before using the practices. Alternatively, you may like to create a small altar on which you place symbolic objects, affirmations, key words, crystals or photographs of beautiful scenery, planets, temples or elements that resonate with that step's particular angel. You might also add a vase of fresh flowers or a statue of an angel.

When your sacred space is ready, dedicate the space to the highest possible good, for the greatest benefit of all who enter there, and call upon any particular angels you choose to guide your work.

You could say something like: "I dedicate this space to work with the angels for the highest purpose and greatest good of all – may all who enter here feel blessed."

My choice of crystals for working with angels is clear quartz for spiritual work, rose quartz for love and heart-centred work, and amethyst for transformation and healing. Lately, though, I have been taking a small bag containing twelve small crystals – six pieces of raw moonstone and six pieces of raw quartz crystal – to workshops. I carried these crystals with me on a retreat to the Holy Land and I believe they are imbued with the special sacred energy of the sites I visited with my group and so add

something unique. It is always good to follow your personal
intuitive guidance about what feels best for you.

Space clearing

If you are concerned that negative energy might be lingering
in your home – perhaps as a result of illness, bereavement or
relationship issues – there are several methods you can use to
cleanse the room before setting up your sacred space.

If the room hasn't been used in a while, you'll need to
physically clean it, removing any clutter, dust and dirt,
and then use incense or a smouldering white sage brush or
smudge stick (you can buy or make your own, most New Age
or crystal shops sell them) to cleanse the air. Go round the
room slowly and waft the smoke and fragrance high into all
the corners and down to the floor, perhaps saying a prayer and
inviting the angels and the Divine, or any other sacred energy
of your choice, to cleanse and purify the room, removing any
negativity that may be lingering there.

You could also call upon Raphael, the Archangel of
Consecration, saying, "Archangel Raphael, I ask you to cleanse,
purify and consecrate this space. Thank you."

Or, if you prefer, try connecting to the elements and four
directions. Something like: "I call upon the powerful energies
of the four directions, Angels of the North, East, South and
West, to the energies of the elements, fire, water, earth and
air, to purify and clear this space, dedicating it to use for the
highest purpose and greatest good. May all who enter here be
blessed. Thank you."

As an alternative to incense or a smudge stick, you can use
the sound vibration of a tuning fork instead. (I might even

repeat the prayers with a tuning fork as well as the smoke and incense if I feel the need.)

There are no rules, as long as the words come from your heart.

PRACTICE 2
Creating sacred space within

Your personal sacred space is always within, so it is important that you return to this place before using any of the practical exercises in this book. To establish this for the first time, use the following steps:

1. Find a quiet place where you'll be undisturbed – such as your newly created sacred space – and make yourself comfortable. Now breathe calmly and deeply, down into your belly, and close your eyes.
2. Focus on the space behind your forehead between your eyebrows, known as the "third eye", where it is said in some Eastern cultures that the soul resides (see illustration, page 28).
3. Now imagine you are walking down some steep steps that lead you into a warm room. There is a comfortable safe space here, perhaps with an armchair for you to sit in. This is your interior safe space, unique to you, where you cannot be disturbed and no one can trouble you. This is where you can pray or communicate with your angels and guides whenever you wish.
4. When you are ready, come back up the steps and return to the present moment.

With practice, you'll find that you can go to your sacred space within a few moments, even when chaos is happening all around you.

Chakras in meditation and healing

Working with the seven energy centres of the body, known as the "chakras", also forms part of the practices in the Seven Steps. Chakra is a Sanskrit word meaning "wheel of light" and derives from the highly trained Indian yogis that observed the chakras as spinning vortexes. It is through this energy that our life force flows, stimulating the endocrine system and helping us maintain a healthy, open balance of body, mind, spirit and soul. As a filter of subtle energies from Earth and Heaven, the chakras also act as conductors, and can help you become more open to receiving and transmitting Angel Light.

PRACTICE 3
Tuning into the seven chakras

Look at the diagram below and note the location of each of the seven chakras, then use the following short meditative exercise to help you tune into the energies of your body and the spectrum of light of the Archangels.

1. Sit comfortably with your spine straight and both feet firmly on the floor. Focusing your attention on your feet, imagine roots from the soles going down into the earth.
2. Taking slow, deep breaths, imagine a bright red mist swirling around your feet, your legs and up to your

7 Crown chakra (violet)

6 Brow (third eye) chakra (indigo)

5 Throat chakra (turquoise)

4 Heart chakra (green)

3 Solar plexus chakra (yellow)

2 Sacral chakra (orange)

1 Root chakra (red)

The seven chakras

hipbones. Connect with this beautiful rich colour and the chakra we call the "root", which rests at the perineum, at the base of the spine, and draws its energy from the Earth's core. Imagine the red colour energizing your blood and all your cells, giving you stamina, courage and resilience.

3. Now, breathing slowly, imagine the red turning to a brilliant bright orange. See this swirling around your pelvis to just under your navel, the "sacral" chakra. This energy centre is essential for your vitality and wellbeing, enabling enjoyment in physical ways and allowing you to move forward in life. Visualize that rich orange colour as

you remind yourself of your ability to care for and cherish your physical presence in the world.

4. The third chakra is the "solar plexus", which brings the colour of sunshine yellow all around your middle, energizing the vital organs for healthy digestion of food and ideas. Sense that yellow colour and imagine bathing in the warming sunshine as you value your qualities and your relationships with others.

5. Now, see the colour changing to bright green. Imagine the swirling coloured light energy moving up and energizing your "heart" chakra, which sits in the middle of your chest and operates on both the physical and emotional aspects of life. Feel into your heart energy, which thrives on love, by thinking of some of your happiest moments, filling your whole self with joy.

6. As the coloured light moves further up your body, it changes to a bright turquoise blue and swirls around your neck, throat, mouth and chin like a beautiful silk scarf. The "throat" chakra directs the life force through integrity and willpower, as well as self-expression and clear communication. Enjoy the sensation of this gorgeous colour surrounding you.

7. Next, imagine the deepest colour of the midnight sky, a deep indigo-purple velvet, gently brushing your forehead. Sense the energy flowing up towards your "brow" or "third eye" chakra, which sits between your eyebrows, seeking meaning, truth and freedom. As you breathe slowly and comfortably, allow this energy to link the life force moving through you for your highest good.

8. Now, see this swirling coloured energy change to a deep violet as it bathes your "crown" chakra, found at the top of your head, in its gorgeous light. Strengthening your

connection to the core of your being, this chakra offers you the bliss of cosmic consciousness, allowing you to feel loved, guided and protected at all times by the angelic forces.

9. As you bask in the rainbow of bright colours for a few moments, imagine that all your chakra centres are strong and clear.

10. Take a deep breath and, with a sense of gratitude, watch as all the colours gently subside as they float back down your body, gradually ending up at your feet before they slowly disappear into the earth.

Your personal ashram

All over the world, and specifically in India, you will find temples or centres, known as "ashrams", dedicated to selfless devotion, spiritual practice and learning. Here you can leave behind the distractions of the material world and spend either several days or several months clearing away your emotional and mental "baggage". The idea is that you find your true self by detaching from everything that isn't actually your own truth. By working in this way, you raise your energy vibration by developing spiritually towards a clearer sense of self-realization, which inevitably leads to inner peace.

Seven Steps into Angel Light may not be an ashram in India, but my hope is that it will help you to create such a space within your own life for you to embark upon your own journey of spiritual development, allowing you to get to know yourself better and reconnect with your inner Angel Light and qualities.

ANGEL PRAYER

Dear Archangels,

In the name of "I AM that I AM" we detach and let go of all energy in truth that is not ours.

We call back to ourselves all energy in truth that is ours and we ask that as it comes back to us it may be dissolved in the Love and the Light.

We call to the seven Archangels and their Legions of Light:

To Archangel Gabriel and the Angels of Communication;

To Archangel Jophiel and the Angels of Illumination and Wisdom;

To Archangel Michael and the Angels of Protection;

To Archangel Raphael and the Angels of Healing;

To Archangel Chamuel and the Angels of Love;

To Archangel Uriel and the Angels of Peace;

And the beloved Archangel Zadkiel and the Angels of Joy.

With gratitude in our hearts we ask you to enter our earthly affairs and bring to us your wonderful heavenly qualities. Give us please the freedom from fear and self-doubt, that we may find in our minds your wisdom and illumination, understanding, inspiration, creativity, knowledge and clearness of sight.

Help us to fully appreciate and enjoy the qualities of giving and receiving unconditional love, to feel compassion, mercy and forgiveness.

Show us how to dissolve the feelings of selfishness, self-condemnation and low self-esteem.

Give us the guidance we need to create inner peace and tranquility in our hearts and minds, with a truly spiritual balance in our humanness.

We ask that with the love and guidance of the Divine, the source of all life, and the help of the angels, we will grow to reach the understanding of true universal Christ consciousness.[6]

As we ask, with honest intent, so it may be so.

Thank you.

Amen.

———————————

STEP 1

AWAKEN TO YOUR SOUL PURP
SELF-UNDERSTANDING WITH ARCHANGEL GABRIEL

"I knew who I was this morning, but I've changed a few
times since then."

Lewis Carroll, *Alice's Adventures in Wonderland*

KEY ANGEL ASSOCIATIONS

Attributes: Communication, Intuition,
Self-knowledge, Awakening, Grounding
Colour: Keeper of the White Flame
Crystals: Celestine, Selenite, Clear quartz,
Moonstone, Diamond
Planetary influences: Moon and Mercury
Day of the week: Wednesday
Element: Ether
Ashram: Mount Shasta, Oregon, USA

Are you ready? You are off on a journey of self-discovery and
this is where you start to collect the tools required for the road
ahead. This first step marks a fresh page, a new beginning. By
the end of it you will have a greater understanding of why you
are here, why you were inspired to seek out the Angel Light
and a clearer vision of your soul's purpose.

This first step also marks the beginning of your journey of communication on all levels with the angelic realms – spiritual, emotional and physical. Here you'll discover the brilliant white Light of Archangel Gabriel. A beautiful angelic being known as the great "Annunciator", Gabriel lights the way – as Divine Messenger, angel of death and rebirth, and instigator of new projects and beginnings.

Even though this Archangel is often referred to as being male, for me Gabriel is a strong and powerfully feminine Light. I call her the "Cosmic Midwife of the Universe". She guides each soul from conception to birth, showering us with blessings of love and gifting us with an inner knowledge of our true soul purpose. This wisdom is within us all, but only with Gabriel's Divine guidance are we are able to remember it.

Guardian of the Moon, she lights the way forward in darkness and whispers messages of hope, encouragement and creative wisdom in our ears. She sows seeds and instigates change. When you connect with Gabriel, you'll discover her Light is pure crystal white, bringing brightness and great joy. The practical exercises in this chapter will show you how to:

- Tune in deeply with your own body; learn to feel what it is telling you about the way you are living your life and how your thought processes are directing you.
- Develop your intuition so that you can start recognizing those internal nudges and external signs that are pointing you in the direction of your soul purpose.
- Understand the events in your own life story that have brought you here – to start the journey to self-knowledge we first have to go back to the beginning.

- Use the root chakra to stay grounded and strengthen the throat chakra to increase your self-expression and willpower.

Opening up the channels of communication

Working with the angels may feel a little daunting at first, but just as we all breathe the same air, are made from the same minerals, elements and water, and tread the same earth, so the angel energies are available to us all. The ways they interact with you, your connection to the Divine and your own spiritual impulse – just like the movement of your body, the colour of your eyes and the shades of your skin – are absolutely unique.

PRACTICE 1
Seeking guidance on your awakening with Gabriel

Use this guided meditation to open up a channel of communication with Gabriel. The questions and childhood reflections will help you to become aware of what you have perhaps lost along the way or simply where your Light is not shining as brightly as it could. Either way, you're likely to see the first glimmerings of your soul purpose emerge after this meditation.

If you need to refresh your memory about using the guided meditations, see Tools for Your Journey (page 17). Or, if you prefer to listen to it as a download, go to: www.AngelLight. co.uk/sevensteps.

1. Get comfortable and, if you choose, spend a few minutes breathing deeply before closing your eyes.

2. Imagine you are breathing in a beautiful beam of white light, like a spotlight, through your right foot. Visualize all the tendons, bones, tissues and muscles in your foot as it is filled with this brightest of lights. Send feelings of gratitude towards your foot, fully appreciating how much you need your feet for standing, walking and moving around. Now breathe in the light into your left foot and, again, imagine your foot full of the white light and send feelings of gratitude towards your foot.

3. Remember your childhood and all the lovely things you did using your two feet – running around, hopping, skipping and jumping. Now pause and consider the following questions, making a note of any answers in your journal:

    • How do I feel about my standing in society?
    • How do I feel about where I stand in my own family?
    • How sure am I that I am on the right spiritual path?
    • Do I know where I came from?
    • Do I know and understand the direction that I chose to follow?

4. With each breath, inhale the light and imagine you can see it rising upwards through your ankles, calves, knees, thighs... Now really feel the light in your legs and your hips. Imagine that the white light is so bright that you can see it moving through the pores of your skin, surrounding the lower half of your body.

5. Now breathe the light through your hips and into your lower abdomen, thanking this whole pelvic area for what it does for you. Appreciate how your cells carry memories and ask yourself: do I feel safe?

6. As you experience the light moving up and through your body, allow yourself to fully relax with every exhalation.

Let go of any anxieties, any tension – watching the light, in your mind's eye, as it fills every part of your abdomen, your lungs, your heart and ribcage, across your shoulders, down through your arms and hands, and out through your fingertips. Send warm thoughts of gratitude towards your hands and your arms and imagine all the things you do with them. Imagine reaching out towards your loved ones – embracing them, holding them close to your heart.

7. Now ask yourself: how ready am I to give and receive pure, unconditional love? Take a note of your answer.

8. Breathe in the light, up through your chest, neck and into your face, allowing it to move through your head and, as the light fills your head, picture some of the most beautiful things that you have ever seen or experienced. Your favourite sounds or music. Beautiful fragrances. Wonderful tastes. Words and gentle whisperings. Be grateful for all the wondrous things that the senses do for you and fill them with light.

9. As your head absorbs the crystal white light, allow it to fill your mind with heavenly purity and its love. Invite and allow it to cleanse and purify anything you may be holding in your thoughts that is not of the purist love.

10. And now, as you see yourself as a being full of pure white light, simply call the name of Archangel Gabriel three times in your mind. Invite the powerful energy of Gabriel to come closer to you, seeing in your mind's eye the brilliant white light associated with this Archangel's presence. Allow yourself to be open to this pure Divine Being of awakening, communication and direction.

11. If you have any questions regarding the direction of your journey ahead, ask them now. Ask, too, whether you are already fulfilling your soul's purpose.

12. Allow the messages to flow through you: as sensations, emotions, pictures or even words. As you ask Gabriel to give you a sense of your direction, sit for a moment in that space and see if you can find it in your heart. You may feel it as a physical sensation (such as a tingle, or change in temperature), or see it in your mind as a vision. You might hear it in words. Trust the messages you are being given. Gently notice, without analysing, whatever comes to you.

13. Sit in this presence absorbing the light and the love for a few minutes. Then, with a sense of heartfelt gratitude, thank Gabriel and know that you are truly loved, releasing the Archangel to move away from you. Consciously focus your awareness on the Light in your own body. Slowly breathe it right down through you and out of the soles of your feet into Mother Earth. Feel it expanding through the pores of your skin into the ether.

14. As you slowly breathe in and out, be aware now of where you are sitting, your feet firmly placed on the ground. Become aware of the weight and heaviness of your body.

15. Breathing slowly, deeply, deliberately, allow yourself to come back to the present moment. Bring yourself into your own space, your own room, and breathe normally. Feel your body: solid, present and fully grounded. Very slowly, when you're ready, open your eyes.

*

I'd suggest making this guided meditation part of your daily practice for the next seven days but, as with all the exercises in this book, there is no time limit. There is no right or wrong way to do it, only the right way for *you* – and this is part of determining a sense of your true self and your soul's fulfilment.

The more often you engage with Gabriel's Light, the more it will help you to trust that the right thing happens just at the right time. To be open to receive just what you need when you need it, to understand and start following your soul calling – whether it's retraining, changing your lifestyle, or bringing more compassion or creativity into your life. Open your eyes and you'll start to see that all those previously unnoticed synchronicities, coincidences or chance meetings offer messages of support from the angels. It might be a loving gesture from another person, a website, a talk or a book that provides motivation and inspiration. Right when you are in need, in that perfect moment. Allow these moments to be signs of Divine love that remind you that you are supported in your endeavours to find your soul purpose.

Use the following affirmation to help remind you to look out for signs that Gabriel's Light is all around you:

My life is a wonderful journey of discovery.
I have faith that I will clearly see the direction
that I need to follow.

Stepping into Gabriel's Light awakens intuition

As you go about your day-to-day life, you may notice that your increased self-awareness prompts other deep senses to awaken too. The angels pick up on your thoughts and desires telepathically, reading the light from your thought forms as they sparkle within your aura. Working with Gabriel in particular encourages the development and use of this powerful intuition or "sixth sense".

Intuition is that deep inner sense of "knowing" that you cannot easily explain. As you become more accustomed to sensing your own Light, you might notice that you are more highly tuned to other people's energy, too, and begin to notice those people that make your Light sparkle and those that depress your inner radiance.

Many people have gifts like this, though they may call them by different names, such as clairvoyance (to "see"), clairsentience (to "feel a presence"), "clairaudient" (to "hear") and "empathic" (to "sense" emotion). These psychic abilities can be developed, but when you align with the powerful universal forces of the Divine and the loving energies of the angelic realms, such psychic qualities will naturally arise as you are inspired to be more compassionate. This drives you to seek more connection with the beauty of the physical world and the wider, more ethereal Universe. As this connection intensifies, so your intuition intensifies too.

This is a really important first step in recognizing and following your soul purpose because you start to notice the different energies around you. For example, you may feel a pain and realize you are sensing someone else's suffering in your own body, empathically yet involuntarily. You will often think of someone just before they send you a message or "know" who is about to call on the phone even before it rings. You may also become more sensitive to the atmosphere, and to other people's energy, as well as becoming more skilful at discerning positive opportunities. Continue to develop your intuition to help you recognize whether Gabriel and the angels are calling you back onto your true path by asking for a clear sign, one that is unique to you, and keep a journal of where and when the answers come to you. So, if you think finding feathers is a sign of angelic assistance, then ask to see a feather in your favourite colour and then be prepared to find one – but not necessarily where you might expect. As you gain confidence in reading the signs you will be able to look back through your notes and decipher the messages with greater clarity.

As Archangel Gabriel is the master of communication, it is useful to establish the strength and capacity of your own spiritual communication, identifying the way the angels are most likely to connect with you. The following "memory" exercise will help you to read the signs and see how best you personally communicate with the angels.

PRACTICE 2
Developing your intuition

In this exercise you'll be accessing a memory by using your "imaginal" self to establish which of your senses is sharpest, and in which way the angels are most likely to communicate with you. So, if you are a visual person it may be that the colours are very bright and you "see" pictures. Or perhaps the smells are strong and easy to recollect, or the sounds are so clearly remembered that you can "hear" them again. Sometimes it is the overall emotion or physical sensation of the memory you will feel. Or it might be one or more, or all; it might be easy or not, but as always there are no rights or wrongs, just your own path.

Whatever you experience, these are an indication of the same types of sensation you will have in the presence of angels or when you are receiving messages from your celestial guides and helpers.

1. Close your eyes and bring to mind a happy memory. It can be recent or from childhood, it doesn't matter when, only that it brings joy. (Try not to think of something that includes a deceased loved one, as this may invoke too

many mixed emotions.) Visualize the memory as clearly as you can. If you can't visualize, don't worry. You will still be able to imagine it in your mind because you were there.

2. Breathing deeply takes that happy memory deep down into your body, your lower abdomen, just below your navel, which in yoga is called the "hara".

3. Feel into the joy of the memory, allowing a smile to show on your face. Take that down into your body, creating a gentle inner smile in your belly. Now focus on the details.

   - Can you see it as a movie playing across your inner vision?
   - Can you see or sense any vivid colours?
   - Do you remember clearly what you were wearing? The fabrics, the comfort (or not) of the clothes against your skin?
   - What is the temperature? Is it warm or cold, dry or wet?
   - Are there any strong smells associated with this memory that spring clearly to your senses?
   - Can you hear any sounds from that occasion? Music or voices? Are they easy to recall?
   - What are the emotions you feel as you remember all of this?

4. Now open your eyes and write down the answers to the above questions in your journal.

5. Finally, take a note of your answer to this question: Which aspects were the easiest to recall? List them, starting with the easiest and ending with the most difficult.

I am blessed with many happy memories from childhood and, like many of my generation, was given so much freedom that most of my memories involve some kind of adventure. But when doing the above exercise it is always the same favourite vivid memory that I turn to. I'm running through the fields in springtime. We lived close to a lovely little place called Kirkby Lonsdale in the Lake District, in the north of England, and I vividly remember running excitedly with arms filled with freshly picked wild daffodils. Farmers would put signs out with the invitation to "Pick your own daffodils", and it was my favourite birthday treat. I'd be wearing a 1960s-style party dress (which was slightly too small and rubbed under my arms), ankle socks and sandals. It didn't matter that the juice from the stems (which I can still clearly smell if I try) dripped onto my pale-blue frock as I ran around picking more and more of these gorgeous, vibrant yellow blooms!

Understanding how you communicate with the angels

We are all different and it is important to learn which method of communication suits you best. If you visualize easily then pictures may pop into your mind's eye when you ask for a visual sign. If you call the angels to come closer you might sometimes smell a fragrance as confirmation, like the smell of roses, strong jasmine or lilies. If you're being warned of something that you need to really pay attention to, you may hear an unusual sound (like someone knocking on the wall), or feel an unusual shiver. When and if this happens, make a mental note of what you were thinking or talking about, what decision you were contemplating or what was happening in your life at the time. Then wait and see if there are more clues indicating a future outcome.

I once heard loud knocking in the night just before I was about to take part in some work with a famous medium. I heard sinister laughter and knew it was a warning that someone or circumstances might take advantage of me in a negative way. I approached the work with caution and, sure enough, it was strenuous and very challenging. Someone else might have cancelled the engagement. I called in the angels, prayed for support and came through the other side very tired but wiser. Like everyone else I have had to learn what works best for me. All of us are a work in progress.

Start to take note in your journal of any strong feelings you have. Don't worry if you don't fully understand their meaning at first – simply becoming aware of them is enough for the time being. You might notice, for example, that certain people or activities provoke certain sensations in your body. Part of learning to tune in and become more self-aware is giving yourself time and space, so whenever possible slow your step, breathe deeply and focus on the task in hand. In this way, you increase your self-awareness and become more alert to your intuition. Use the following affirmation to support you as you go about your day:

I trust in my ability to have clear insight, as I open myself up to the flow of universal energy and communicate with all my senses.

From awakening to clarity of purpose

Before we move on and start exploring the past in order to understand what circumstances and events brought you here, I'd like to share two important tools with you. They focus on your wellbeing and will provide you with the strong foundations and willpower you'll need as you seek out and follow your soul purpose:

- Root chakra grounding.
- Strengthening self-expression using the throat chakra.

Growing strong roots: grounding

Archangel Gabriel is mainly associated with the throat chakra, the centre of communication and will. However, this angelic force is also closely linked to the root chakra because she "over-lights" our entry to the world at birth and working with her Light enables us to become conduits of Divine energy. Our aim is therefore to create a strong, clear communication with the angels while also balancing the root chakra so that we feel safe enough to stand our ground.

This is important because in order to express your highest truth and open the "third eye"[1] to the light, you will need to open the upper chakras (see Tools for Your Journey, page 27). But first you need to strengthen the lower chakras (starting from the root and working upwards) or you may feel off balance or floaty. Ways to ground yourself include meditating on the root chakra, walking in nature or feeling the earth beneath your feet.

PRACTICE 3
Root chakra grounding

Use the following practice anytime you want to feel more grounded and especially before any of the guided meditations that follow.

1. Stand with your feet shoulder-width apart. Breathe deeply and focus on your feet.
2. Feeling the soles of your feet connecting with the floor, imagine that there are roots going from this point down deep into the ground, right to the centre of the Earth.
3. Visualize energy coming up through these roots from Mother Earth and feel a sense of gratitude as she supplies all the nourishment our bodies require while we meditate.
4. As you get further into your meditation practice you'll find that you are able to easily visualize the Divine Light coming down through your body into the Earth and the Earth energies coming up into your body.

Strengthening self-expression with the throat chakra

When we are honourable, truthful and reliable – always sticking by what we say and know to be true and expressing ourselves openly – we strengthen the throat chakra. And when we have a strong resilient container of energy in the throat chakra, it becomes a powerful force for the spirit, acting as a conduit for Divine guidance to be carried from our crown to our hearts. It also acts the other way, taking our heartfelt honest desires to the crown for connection with the Divine and the angelic realms.

More often than not, however, it is the act of *expressing* our truth that we often find tricky. Even if we are gentle, kind and sensitive, we might be timid in expressing our real truth for fear of rejection or upsetting others. This affects not only our speech and integrity but also the strength of our will. We may, for example, find it difficult to say "no" to things that are harmful to us. Whether it is is idle gossip or conforming to unrealistic expectations, we think we are being "nice" by not raising any objections to the behaviour of other people around us, but actually we are harming ourselves – mind, body and soul.

Working on strengthening the throat chakra will help you to strengthen your will in following your soul purpose. To do this make a commitment to be as truthful as you can in all situations. Be careful what you say about others too, as gossip hurts you as much as it hurts them. You may also need to watch your levels of eating, drinking alcohol and smoking, as well as all drugs (whether prescription or recreational).

Listen to your true inner guidance for signs from the angels, speak clearly and mean what you say. Using the following affirmation will help support you:

I live and speak my truth, trusting and knowing that my communication comes from the core of my inner being.

Working out future soul purpose from the past

Feeling grounded and being able to express your truth are both vital tools for the next and final section of the first step: investigating the past to discover what brought you to this point where you want something more from life. This type of self-enquiry can be hugely rewarding but also very challenging (and sometimes draining). Guilt, remorse and blame (including self-blame) have no place in this process. You will be travelling purely as an observer, without judgement, simply accepting the past as something that happened and looking for the gems of learning within it. And, remember, you can call on Gabriel's brilliant white Light at any time to help you step into self-awareness without self-blame or judgement.

Going back in time and revisiting the things you were told by others, or actions you took as a result of what you'd learned, will help you to work out *why* you think you are who you are.

PRACTICE 4
Creating a timeline

Take your time as you carry out this exercise. You can add to it whenever you choose and we will come back to it in later chapters, so keep it safe.

1. Draw a line horizontally on a piece of paper and mark it vertically with equal divisions to represent seven-year stages of your life, the first of which marks the period from conception to age seven. (Before you were born your mother may have had experiences during her pregnancy that affected you, and we shall be looking at this further in Step 4, when we'll do some deeper chakra work together.)
2. You can now be as artistic and creative as you like. Feel free to use words and descriptions if you prefer but I'd suggest devising little symbols and using different coloured pens to mark significant events that happened at specific times to make you the unique and wonderful person you are.
3. Write down or draw these events under the line if the experience had a negative affect, or above the line if it was positive. So, for example, if a sibling or grandparent (or anyone else you loved dearly) left you at any point (including while you were in your mother's womb), write or draw it underneath the line. Connect the word or picture to the main horizontal timeline with a vertical

line. How long or short that line is will depend on how much you feel the experience had a detrimental effect. Positive experiences, such as falling in love, passing an exam, learning to ride a bike or drive a car, or travelling somewhere exciting, should be marked above the line using the same method.

Try not to overanalyse the events, or judge yourself, while you compile the timeline. Simply reflect and record them. You may find this experience quite cathartic when you do this for the first time, and, even if you have done it before, I encourage you to do it again anyway.

Key events to note include: moving home, the birth of a sibling, separation within a family, changing or leaving school, any serious illness (yours or of those close to you), travel, close relationships/marriage, divorce/separation, the births of your children, and any achievements, accomplishments or qualifications, whether academic, artistic, sporting or otherwise.

It is also a good idea to include any religious or spiritual experiences, such as a first visit to a church or temple, any times of deep questioning, near-death experiences or strong spiritual sensations. Note down whether or not you attended a secular or a faith school and when you first learned about your particular religious background, if relevant. Then note if and when you made any alternative decisions about your faith upbringing, your spirituality, or, if there was none, when you think you first became interested.

Looking back in this way, you may now be able to pinpoint certain events and experiences that determined how you arrived where you are now. You may also start to more fully understand what ambitions or driving forces are leading you where you are going, giving you a fuller picture that allows you to create a map for the future.

On the other hand, this exercise might have also brought up more uncertainty about your spiritual path. If so, please don't worry: that is common, and as you build on the flow of energy emerging (and being created by you) along the Seven Steps, your unique spiritual impulse will start to emerge more clearly too. For example, you might get a deep sense of knowing that some things no longer feel "right". This is because you are tapping into your own instinctive truth, and possibly beginning to see that even though some of the dogma you were taught many years before can still have a residual effect, it no longer serves you. Many people are drawn to the energy of angels because they understand these beings as a gentler, less intrusive presence than organized religion. Angelic beings are nonetheless as inseparable from the Divine (whoever or whatever that means for you) as you are – we are all part of the same universal creation or consciousness.

Very often it is a lack of spiritual practice or denial of our spirituality that challenges us most. A deep unnamed fear or sense of separation can play out in many forms of neurosis. There are a multitude of theories, from psychologists to theologians. Some say it stems from a neonatal fear of separation from our mother, others a fear of damnation and separation from the Divine. But, in truth, we cannot ever be separated because we are all part of the same Divine creation.

It is perfectly natural to have anxious moments during this process of self-reflection, where fear creeps in and seems to take over. When this happens just stop what you are doing, clear your mind and concentrate on your breath. Feel your feet on the ground, breathe slowly and deeply into the hara, your lower abdomen, to centre yourself. This will bring you back into alignment with the life force and the light and will allow you to operate from a place of love, not fear.

We cannot begin to understand the full extent of our spiritual connections to the Divine source of love – no one can. But, by offering generosity of spirit, making gestures of unsolicited kindness, expressing genuine interest and gratitude, helping those who need it wherever possible, offering prayers and blessings regularly on behalf of other people as well as ourselves, we are connecting to the universal energy of pure love.

In Step 4, we'll look at how gratitude and love affects our karma, but for now, with the help of the beneficent Archangel Gabriel, we have begun the process of recognizing our personal pathway, of learning how to resonate with our true spiritual impulse.

> The clarion call of the angels touches our soul, invites us back into the Light and reminds us that we are all spiritual beings, and that this is, in spite of everything we might deem to be imperfect, a very beautiful world.

Readying yourself for the journey ahead

Having now taken the first step into the Angel Light, how are you feeling? We live in a frantic world, where some days it can be difficult to find even five minutes' downtime away from the rush. But in order to follow this path, in order to fully step into your Light, remember that you will need to nurture yourself – mind, body and spirit – and remain balanced and strong. By this I mean consciously achieving a happy balance between your work life, your family life and your spiritual life, between health and money, love and charity, work and play.

Once you become more aware of the need to prioritize your health and wellbeing, you can develop strategies for putting that understanding into action. This might include bodywork – such as massage, reflexology or yoga – eating a nutritious diet and taking exercise. You can call in the angels to guide you towards those activities that are good for you, and assist you in reorganizing your schedule to fit it all in. Archangel Gabriel's Light is wonderful for showing you the way.

In terms of nurturing your spiritual development, the simplest way to do this is through meditation, connecting with nature, and doing the things that make your heart sing – whether that be listening to music, dancing, walking, being with animals or children, laughing or playing.

You know when you are out of balance: the aspect of life that is draining you will leave you feeling exhausted and overwhelmed. If you have no energy or enthusiasm for something, it is time to take a break and reassess. When you are happy and well, you are in good balance. The physical body you see and feel is not all you are, and to maximize your Light you need to take full responsibility for your own health (on all levels) and let go of all blame and excuses.

The same is true of developing your soul. There are no "quick fixes". No matter what any teacher or guru says, no one but you can "accelerate your ascension process", "realign your DNA" or mend your broken heart, however much money you are willing to pay. We are each responsible for our own decisions, actions and outcomes. Use the following affirmation to support you on your journey:

I stand in my own power, taking full responsi-
bility for my thoughts, words and actions.

Reaching this point of self-awareness can often enable the first great changes to take place and bring a cataclysmic shift in energy. We begin to understand that although other people affect us, we are in fact in control of our own lives. Just like becoming good at sport or playing the piano, we know we have to put in the practice; we realize that in order to be happy and fulfilled we have to do the work. We are responsible for the stories we tell to others and to ourselves. By taking full ownership of our decisions, we can rewrite our stories, make a fresh start and begin again, creating anything we want to.

DAILY PRAYER

Dear Archangel Gabriel,

I call upon your powerful presence.

I thank you from my heart for your guidance and I ask to be shown in ways that I will clearly understand how best to pursue my soul's intention.

Gabriel, please surround me in your brilliant white Light and purify my thoughts and deeds that I may communicate my truth with clarity and purpose.

Let my eyes always look clearly ahead on the road you wish me to tread, that I might not be tempted away by distractions.

Protect me from lies and falsehood, and help me to learn discernment that I might avoid deception whenever I meet it.

Thank you.

Amen.

STEP 2

SEEK YOUR INNER WISDOM AND CREATIVITY
DELVING INTO THE MYSTERY
WITH ARCHANGEL JOPHIEL

"The most beautiful experience we can have is the mysterious. It is the fundamental emotion that stands at the cradle of true art and true science."

Albert Einstein, *The World As I See It*

KEY ANGEL ASSOCIATIONS

Attributes: Wisdom, Creativity, Inspiration, Illumination, Enlightenment, Spiritual Nourishment, Mystery

Colour: Keeper of the Yellow Flame

Crystals: Citrine, Amber, Topaz

Planetary influences: Saturn and Jupiter

Day of the week: Monday

Element: Fire

Ashram: Above Lanchow, China

Having now experienced the brilliance of Archangel Gabriel's Light, Step 2 goes on to explore an array of mystical (and often surprising) experiences and practices that will inspire and enlighten you on the next stage of your spiritual journey.

Whether you can feel it or not, your personal vibration is already changing and you may find that you now have a strange thirst for knowledge, particularly relating to your Higher or true Self. You may, for example, notice a powerful desire to be alone more than usual, or find yourself drawn to mix with other like-minded people who are also seeking a more spiritual way of living. Connecting to the warmth of Jophiel's great golden Light will help you to feel more deeply into this spiritual space.

Jophiel[1] is one of the original Archangels of creation and transmits Divine inspiration to one and all. Working with Jophiel's Light can help you release any blockages that are holding you back from bringing spiritual practices into your life. He shows you that there is beauty in everything. And when you open your heart and mind to fully experience this beauty, Jophiel's Light guides you towards a point of clarity and deeper understanding. You will begin to get a clearer picture of how everything in the Universe is energy. He will show you that everything is connected and interwoven like threads of a tapestry – a fabulously exciting cosmic order, a Divine co-creation – that includes you.

When you connect with Jophiel's energy, you'll discover a warm, bright golden light that brings inspiration, creativity and spiritual nourishment. The practical exercises in this chapter will show you how to:

- Connect with your inner wisdom and re-remember creative practices that motivate you and allow you to be in flow with life.

- Bring more sacredness into daily life through simple rituals that will provide spiritual nourishment.

- Learn how to recognize and embrace more mystical experiences in your life.

- Explore the differences between religion and spirituality. Let go of any judgements about yourself by understanding that your own spiritual impulse lies in the practices that bring you most illumination.

- See the beauty in everything and so awaken to yourself as part of the mystery of creation.

- Develop practices that will bring you ever closer to blissful contentment.

Delving into your spiritual impulse and creativity

You might initially wonder what the connection is between creativity and spiritual connection, but in the same way that we can so easily get caught up in the busyness of life that we lose a healthy life balance, so too can we forget the creative and spiritual practices that bring us joy.

PRACTICE 1
Seeking wisdom and creativity with Jophiel

Stepping into Jophiel's Light will help you tap into your internal wisdom and remember all these creative endeavours that, when practised, allow you to become absorbed in the moment and, in so doing, quiet the thinking mind.

If you need to refresh your memory about using the guided meditations, see Tools for Your Journey (page 17), or, if you prefer to listen to it as a download, go to: www.AngelLight.co.uk/sevensteps.

1. Get comfortable and, if you choose, spend a few minutes breathing deeply before closing your eyes.
2. Think of your favourite colour. Breathe it into your body. Breathe out any tension or anxieties you may have. With each out-breath, allow your neck and shoulders to relax. Allow your arms to sit comfortably on your thighs, with your palms facing upwards. Give yourself permission to truly relax.
3. Imagine your favourite colour passing down through your body, into your arms and your legs, until the colour comes out through your skin. See yourself sitting as a bright being of brilliant colour.
4. In your imagination see your whole being surrounded by golden sunshine light. Feel that light. Feel its warmth. Sense it around your face, on your skin. And, through your closed eyes, see the light become brighter and brighter.
5. Visualize the sun and just think about how strong that sunlight is. As you embrace the light around you, think about how bright, how beautiful, how warm, how life-giving sunlight is. As you think about the strength of the sun's light if you were to look directly at it, try to imagine how much stronger the light from the Divine must be.
6. Now imagine walking through a beautiful garden. Look around you and find somewhere to sit. As you sit down, notice the flowers, the trees, the butterflies moving around you, feel the sunshine on your skin. Perhaps you can smell a fragrance. Allow yourself to enjoy the freedom

of being on your own in this special sacred place. Immerse yourself in the beauty and wonder of the garden – the wonder of creation.

7. As you look around the garden you see a very tall, bright being walking towards you. As he continues to approach you, the light is almost blinding. The angel tells you telepathically that he or she represents the angels of the realm belonging to creativity, governed by the Angel Jophiel.

8. Ask the angel to inspire you, to illuminate your mind – to give you a message that will help you in your creative powers, to give you a sense of your very own creativity, your own wisdom. As pictures, colours, words or sensations come to you, make a mental note but try not to analyse them.

9. Thank the angel, and fully bathe in this beautiful golden light. Feel a sense of gratitude in your heart as the angel then walks on by.

10. Bring into your mind all the beautiful, creative or artistic things that you have been part of or that have deeply impacted you. Allow them to fill your memory and appreciate that you too take part in the co-creation of our Universe. Now think about how creativity comes to you in your own personal life: what creative pursuits bring you joy?

11. Think of some of the most beautiful places that you have ever visited. Now take yourself to your favourite place, a place full of happy memories. Think of the colours, sounds, textures and fragrances. Allow yourself to feel the joy and warmth of being with that memory, and breathe it down into your body as an inner smile and a lasting joy. You might like to stay with that moment for a little while.

12. Feeling the joy of that memory, take yourself back to the garden where you imagined sitting among the flowers, trees, butterflies and birds. Give yourself a little more time to recognize a sense of inner peace and tranquillity.

13. Breathing slowly, deeply, deliberately, allow yourself to be back in the present moment. Bring yourself into your own space, your own room, and breathe normally. Feel your body: solid, present and fully grounded. Very slowly, when you're ready, open your eyes.

Finding creative inspiration

After experiencing Jophiel's Light, you may feel inspired to take up a new or former artistic outlet. It could be anything from painting to amateur dramatics, writing poetry or visiting the theatre. It could mean creating something new in your life, for example redecorating a room in your home or landscaping an outdoor space. However you feel called to explore your creativity, it is important to honour that aspect of yourself. This is self-care in action and can help you activate your soul purpose. Jophiel's Light inspires this within you and spending time on creative projects will help you feel, and radiate, a more joyful and lighter energy. If you are still unsure what creative outlets might inspire your journey, sit quietly and reflect on the following questions:

- What brought me joy and made my heart sing as a child?
- Where and how do I feel drawn to be creative?

Now spend a little time working out how you can bring more aspects of creativity into your daily life. This will be easier for some of you than others – particularly if you have a young family, a demanding career or elderly relatives to care for (or all of these). However, try to allocate at least a little time each week for something creative. We may not all write or paint, but some of us love to cook, knit, read, potter in the garden, dance or play music. Even buying flowers for yourself and brightening up your home can be a creative act.

Bringing the sacred to life with ritual can also help you welcome more creativity in, as these "special" moments in time will help you to pause and become conscious. Of course, whether you realize it or not, we all cherish rituals and often consider them sacred. For example, sending birthday cards, decorating a cake with candles, kissing loved ones hello and goodbye, or relishing those few moments with a cup of tea before starting work: these are all sacred rituals in their own right, and you can probably think of many more that are particular to you. But when you *consciously* add ritual to your life, you weave in the Golden Thread of Divine Love (see Tools for Your Journey, page 16). Creating sacred rituals doesn't have to be complicated or lengthy. For example:

- Stepping out of bed, you might greet the day by saying, "Thank you for another day, and blessings to the day ahead and to whoever I meet."
- Opening the blinds or drapes, you might like to consciously welcome the sunlight into your home.
- Lighting a candle, you might give thanks for all the support of your ancestors.

- Before eating a meal, you might silently give thanks to all those who have grown, gathered, prepared and cooked the food, and to Mother Earth for nurturing it.
- Before retiring to bed, you might say a short prayer of thanks.

Seeking out the mystery: Mysticism

Now that you've reconnected with creative practices and begun to inject more sacred moments into your life, you will find that the "aha" moments follow rapidly. However, as you start to experience more magical and mysterious moments in daily life, you may also find that it awakens a deep desire to know more about what the "Divine" actually is.

Sometimes we seem to step right into the Light and become overexcited by it, accepting everything we read or hear about it with blind faith. Or, there may be an inclination to look for more profound answers, a heightened consciousness and a deep sense of knowing that we already walk alongside angels.

There is a certain magical essence found in every faith and world religion, as each has some word or practice for attaining ascension or a higher state of being. All of these practices, whether personal or within a community, help to raise the vibration of humanity as a whole. There is much talk nowadays of "Global Healing", and we'll be delving more into how to help heal the planet and others in Step 4.

For now, focusing on the yellow brilliance and brightness of Archangel Jophiel's Light, a positive, powerful energy raises your vibration – not just because you are gaining knowledge, but because you are absorbing the Light of the Divine Source. This is the meaning of "en-Light-en-ment": taking in the light and allowing it to become part of your whole being. This Divine creative energy is available to anyone who seeks it, and you can tap into it whenever you need to by simply closing your eyes and calling Jophiel's name three times: "Jophiel, Jophiel, Jophiel, as I step into your powerful loving Light so Divine creative energy flows and inspires me to take my part in co-creating this beautiful world."

The phenomenon of the mystical experience is not related to a particular religion and not concerned with beliefs and doctrines, but with a natural state of consciousness, experienced by all cultures, at all times throughout history and by followers of every religion and none.

Mysticism has been described as the spiritual connection to the Divine – an experience, feeling or sensation that cannot be explained and that can never tell the whole story. It might be simpler to think of Mysticism as an umbrella term for all sorts of different spiritual and religious experiences.

Pause now and think of any events in your life that in some way felt mystical. It could be seeing a surprisingly clear and beautiful rainbow, taking a ride in a hot-air balloon, witnessing a breathtaking view from the top of a mountain or gazing at the stars. All these experiences, though maginificent, are not in themselves mystical. Yet at some point the awe and wonder hit your senses and the experience is transformed into something else, something more. It touches your heart because you see a different, deeper Divine quality in the experience.

When my father, Fred Astell, was 15, he set off on his bike with his brother for a few days' camping in the Lake District in the north of England. Having cycled all the way from Hertfordshire, they set up camp quite late and my father decided that he wanted to sleep under the starlit sky. This was just before the outbreak of World War II. There was no light pollution and so he was able to look up to a clear velvety sky that was full of stars. He was fascinated by astronomy and was able to name all the visible planets and constellations, so the circumstances and conditions were perfect for him. This was a truly beautiful and joyful experience in and of itself, but what happened next was a completely different kind of experience. As my father lay gazing heavenwards, the stars began to move slowly across the sky. As he stared more attentively, they formed an image of the face of Jesus Christ. After staring in awe for what seemed like hours, the picture was indelibly printed in his mind. As a result of this vision, this magical and mystical experience, he understood that he had some kind of strong connection with Jesus.

His parents had always encouraged his pursuit of the sciences at school and were not particularly religious themselves, so he had no deep knowledge of the Bible or Christianity other than his school education. But he knew in his heart and deep within his soul that somehow, in some way, Jesus was of significant importance to him and would have a great influence on his life. He had a sense that his life would be somehow affected by this celestial vision. As a result, what was at first simply a wonderful and beautiful event became a mystical experience.

PRACTICE 2
Noticing Mysticism

The following exercise is designed to help you recognize and encourage more mystical experiences in your life. You can then add them to the timeline that you created in Step 1 (see Practice 4, page 48).

1. Sitting quietly, focus on your breath for a few moments before inviting in the Light of Jophiel by calling his name three times (see "Tools for Your Journey", page 17).

2. Visualize being bathed in his golden Light before recollecting all the occasions in your life when you experienced true beauty or moments of complete wonder. These will be unique to you, but they may involve sights that took your breath away or times that filled your heart with joy. For example:
   - Sitting on a rock looking out to sea
   - Flying in an aeroplane for the first time, seeing the clouds from the aircraft window as you rise above them
   - Climbing a mountain and looking back at the view
   - Cloud watching
   - Bird watching
   - Playing with your children

3. Add these experiences to your timeline.

4. Now think of any other experiences that you may have found slightly odd or extraordinary. Things you have seen, heard or felt that you simply cannot explain. It might be a sensation, like someone was touching your hair, that felt otherworldly. It may be a voice speaking to you, a fleeting sense of a past life or déjà vu. You may have been sitting quietly by a tree and felt its energy passing to you, or perhaps you have been able to see the aura around someone (before you understood what it was). Add experiences like these to your timeline.

5. Then, scaling it up a little, consider whether you have had any "mysterious" experiences – mystical events you can't understand or explain but that leave you in a wonderful state of "bliss". It could be hearing music as you gaze at

the stars, having clear visions that are far too real to be dreams, witnessing the appearance of orbs or bright lights, or sensing or even seeing an angel. Add these to your timeline too.

Some people experience mystical events all their lives and may even be seeing fairies, angels and nature devas on a regular basis, but the majority do not. Try not to judge such things as imaginary, or rate whether they were actually mystical or not, simply add them into your timeline, wherever in your life they occurred. It is important to understand that even though some inexplicable visions or sensations can be spontaneous, occuring without any "trying" at all, creating space in your busy life will increase the likelihood of them happening.

I have sometimes found that intense prayer or deep breathing, especially in a sacred place or on consecrated ground (such as a temple, church, cathedral or stone circle), can bring some of these sensations. Regular spiritual practice such as meditation and prayer will also enable you to develop an inner silence where the most profound and enlightening sparks of wisdom are likely to emerge.

My own "mystical" experience of an angel felt truly out of this world. It came shortly after I had split up with my first husband in 1998 and I was living in a studio apartment in east London. I had been reading a prayer and invocation for healing with the angels that really moved me, by an author named Eileen Elias Freeman. I found myself in tears as I read the prayer out loud and called out to the angels: "I have dedicated my life to working

with you yet I can't see you. Please, why don't you show yourself
to me?"

Then, as I put the book down, I saw a huge white shape
approaching the French doors. I stood up and walked towards
the balcony and felt the most powerful physical sensation,
which I can only describe as love, in every cell of my body. My
heart felt like it might burst as what appeared to be a white
cloud came closer and closer. As the vision became clearer, I saw
the unmistakable shape of an angel. I felt a strong masculine
energy and an inexplicable sense of recognition. I knew him and
he knew me.

He was wearing a long white gown and had two massive
pairs of wings: one pair folded behind his back and the other
pointed upwards like brush strokes towards the sky. As he
approached, he became larger and larger and I could clearly see
the light fabric of his white gown blowing in the breeze around
his bare feet. His face was framed by shoulder-length white
hair but it was impossible to see any features because the light
radiating from his face was as bright as the sun. As I moved
closer towards the window, with tears streaming down my face,
the angel held out his hands and arms to me in a gesture of
giving and receiving. It was as though he was waiting to hold
my hands – as if he knew I so wanted to go with him, but knew
I must stay.

Then, as mysteriously as he appeared, he slowly turned and
drifted away. Then I thought my heart was going to break: I
couldn't believe how painful it was to see him leave. As I watched
him go, a huge pink heart appeared in the sky – the brightest
pink I have ever seen, and a perfect sweetheart shape. It was
a symbol of love to remind me that we are all so loved, there is
nothing in our world as important as the giving and receiving of
love. No words were spoken, there was no fanfare of trumpets or

choral voices, but the angel left me his signature, which was as unmistakable as the vision itself.

This experience left me feeling many strange emotions. The power, depth and strength of my angel experience and the overwhelming sense of love was more intense than I had experienced before or since. There are no words to describe it fully.

Understanding your spiritual impulse

In Buddhism, meditation practices bring an altered state that connects the practitioner to the bliss of emptiness, allowing them to be free from all the suffering created by the anxieties and neuroses of the human mind. In Hinduism, a similar mystical connection to the Divine, called "Brahma", is sought through many different strands of yoga.

Achieving this altered state doesn't have to be part of a religious process, but an experiential method of self-study. Religions seek to define what we should believe, while spiritual practices such as stretching, meditation and breathing exercises may be practised by everyone, whether they regard themselves as spiritual, agnostics or members of a particular faith.

It really doesn't matter if you don't experience an altered state when on this search, as long as you understand what it is, and are expressing your spirituality and creativity. However, it may be that you feel some judgement about exploring your spirituality, perhaps due to your upbringing, and this may be holding you back. Spend some time answering this self-enquiry: what is religion to me?

Let's go a little deeper into understanding this idea of a spiritual impulse – not so that you can adopt a label, or put yourself in a category or box, but to deepen your understanding of who you are, and see where you feel you might fit.

We are all unique and have our own personal perspective on everything. All the ideas we share with others will be coloured by our past experiences, our gender, race, religious background, education, social group and ancestral beliefs. The following three-part exercise can help you reflect on where you sit in relation to some of the ideas you might not have thought about for a while, if at all. It's designed to help you truly know and value your opinions, and understand how your unique perspective helps to co-create your own reality.

PRACTICE 3
Exploring spiritual bubbles[2]

Use this self-reflection exercise to feel into your spiritual impulse and understand what type of spiritual practices will be most helpful to you. Remember: there are no rules. Also, your opinions might change as you work through the book so keep your notes somewhere safe – perhaps in a journal – so that you can revisit them.

1. Devotion vs wisdom
First, imagine a horizontal line. At one end is a bubble with the word "Devotion" in it; at the the other, the word in a second bubble is "Wisdom". Where do you think you stand between the two ends of this spiritual scale?

If you have devotional practice, you might include prayers, hymns, spiritual music and sacred ritual in your daily life. You may petition saints or deities, talk to angels, the Divine, the Holy Spirit, Jesus or one or more of the Ascended Masters with a sense of devotion, gratitude and love. You are communicating with someone or something else, and they are listening to you.[3] If this describes your practice or belief, you would place yourself in the Devotion bubble.

Altenatively, you may believe that in some way the Divine is in everything and within us all, though there is still a sense in which you are talking to someone who is listening. In this case, you'd be somewhere in the middle of the scale.

For those at the other end, in the opposite bubble, being non-devotional doesn't mean that you don't believe. You may believe that we are part of the entire Universe, that we are all one, so your understanding will come through silence and meditation to empty and clear the mind. This form of being at peace within comes with practice, and that understanding and wisdom will bring you in tune with an infinite Universe or Source rather than a God or the Divine. In the Hindu system the word for this is *Njani*.

With this distinction between devotional love vs wisdom, you could say we are talking about heart vs head. With Jophiel, however, we are working with both love and wisdom because his creative energy is both. On a practical level, this might mean that you believe in transcending the day-to-day mundaneness of life by adopting a regular meditation or yoga practice (like Buddhism or certain types of self-realization yoga), or spending time each day in prayer, or somewhere in between, or both.

You can be at either end of the scale or somewhere in the middle: there is no right or wrong, just your own truth.

2. Manifest vs unmanifest

Now visualize a second horizontal line with a bubble at each end as you reflect on another two very different and opposite aspects of spiritual belief – "manifest" and "unmanifest".

Read through the following descriptions and then take a few moments to reflect and ask yourself: where am I on this scale?

If you live your spiritual life through the material world, everything you can see around you in physical form, then you are on the "manifest" end of the spectrum. You believe wholeheartedly that we were created in the true image of the Divine, and that in the presence of mankind, and also in nature and in all natural beauty, you have proof that the Divine is "manifested" in everything around you.

Alternatively, you may not need to physically see or touch things to prove your beliefs; there are some things you just accept even though you can't prove it in material terms. This belief that the Divine is outside of and beyond everything you can see is at the other end of the spectrum, in the "unmanifest" bubble.

Where do you sit on the scale? At either end, or somewhere in between the two bubbles? And remember: there are no right or wrong answers – this is just about better understanding your spiritual impulse.

3. Extrovert vs introvert

The final two bubbles I'd like you to visualize again represent opposite ways of being: extroverted or introverted. Where would you place yourself on a spectrum between the two?

From a spiritual perspective, you are an extrovert if you re-energize when you meet up with groups of like-minded people who inspire and nurture you in an atmosphere of sharing and togetherness. If your energy is lifted by group activites, such as workshops, for example, or you enjoy singing in a community, such as a choir or church congregation, you could be called "social" or "communitarian".

If on the other hand you find nurture in solitude and re-energize in the essence of stillness, you would place yourself right at the opposite end of the spectrum, in the introvert bubble. This doesn't mean you always need to be alone, but that this is where you need to go to build up and replenish your energy. So, for example, an introvert who is more devotional might prefer to go into an empty church to pray, or might reach a peak of high spiritual devotion by walking to the top of a mountain and sitting in prayer with nature. Most people would find they need a little of each. Where do you think you sit on the scale?

Perhaps you resonate with all of the above, or just a bit of both. Either way, try to place yourself somewhere along that line, just to add to your map of "self-awareness". There are no right or wrong answers: it's not about "pigeon-holing" but understanding how you feel comfortable expressing and exploring your spirituality.

When you engage your questioning mind and ask, "Where am I in all of this?", you start to understand more about how you operate and what spiritual experiences you need to seek out. The above exercise is not only an interesting one; it can also help you overcome judgements that may have been holding you back from exploring more spiritual pathways.

For example, if you had routinely rejected all forms of formal religion but place yourself nearer the "devotion", "manifest" and "extrovert" bubbles, then you might need to seek out a like-minded community to help you explore and celebrate your spirituality.

Wherever you are on the spectrum, I strongly suggest that you seek out, or revisit, religious experiences, such as visiting a temple, church or synagogue. Take yourself into nature and meditate, or listen to inspirational or choral music. You don't need to "buy in" to any of these experiences – simply do them as an intrepid explorer as a way of opening your mind to the Divine, whatever that might mean to you.

The Light of Archangel Jophiel brings amazing moments of clarity to help you shine a light on who you are and what you know.

Seeking out the Golden Thread

Wouldn't it be good if there was more tolerance in the world? I sense a real importance in making an effort to understand other beliefs, even when we don't necessarily believe them ourselves. We are now in the most exciting of times, when we can research and compare any of the world's religions and belief systems, but do we really understand the symbolism? Having some knowledge of different religious customs can help us to release prejudice and judgements about things that we don't understand. This in turn helps us to let go of our fears (whether silent or spoken) about other people or entities. Often the reason we tend to pass judgement about other people, their dress or expression of faith, is because we have an underlying fear of the unknown.

But when we break down the elements of the world religions, although we may find big differences in the doctrine itself, we also discover a deep-rooted mutual belief in respect, consideration and love. Love is what could be called the Golden Thread in the tapestry we call life.

When we open ourselves to the more mystical side of life, we change the way we see things. The light of love becomes both the destination and the path to transcendence. When we begin to really know love, we will know the One-ness of all things. And when we begin to know that we are all One, we will know real love.

Use the following affirmation to help support you on your exploration:

I see, and am part of, the Golden Thread of Love in all things, running through all beliefs, all faiths, all pathways leading into the Light.

Co-creating with your world and with spirit

Whether you have a particular faith or not, tuning into Jophiel's Light can help you get to know your innermost spiritual nature. As you consider your connection to the Angel Light, and begin to realize how everything is interconnected, this helps to develop a compassion that opens and develops your heart through good times and bad. A deepened sense of spirituality enables you to develop personal integrity, brings balance, realigns all aspects of ourselves, allows ennhanced enjoyment, enables liberation from suffering and increases wellbeing. Boldly recognizing and developing a determination to live and be as spiritual as you can be is about connection to the wider world.

This chapter invites you to engage with all the extra-ordinary and challenging experiences in your life with an understanding that a spark of goodness will inevitably come out of them. Sometimes people don't know that they have a deep spirituality until they need it, so use this step as an invitation to sit and "feel" – even if it is a painful and challenging experience that you don't understand. There will be sparks in every situation that can be interpreted to inspire you to follow a more spiritual life.

In the last exercise in this step, I'll ask you to step into your Higher Self and experience a deeper sense of what it feels like to be part of the glorious Angel Light. It will reinforce the practices and learning of Step 1, and stimulate your growing sense of inner wisdom. Once you become comfortable with this, all the while developing greater self-awareness in the knowledge that each of us is part of the Divine, you will be able to explore and redefine more of the experiences that have shaped your spiritual journey so far. Deepening these memories of people and places, seeking out the special moments and challenges that have shaped your life so far, can also help to define your future. Your unique story is yours to create and yours to tell. It is the journey of your soul, and by tapping into your Higher Self you can redefine the outcome in a more satisfying and fulfilling way than you ever thought possible.

PRACTICE 4
Becoming aware of the universal wisdom

This exercise will develop your intuition and help you to trust in your inner wisdom so that you're able to interpret and use any messages that emerge to map out and define your future path. You'll need your journal and a pen, as you'll be adding more information to the timeline that you started in Step 1 (see Practice 4, page 48).

1. Sit for a moment and imagine yourself growing larger and larger into a gigantic, brightly shining cosmic being – so large that you could hold the Earth in one of your hands.

2. As you look upon the Earth lovingly, imagine that you are sitting among all the brilliant stars, planets, moons and suns that make up the cosmos.

3. Reflect that this Earth in your hands is only one tiny particle of a great, never-ending, star-filled Universe that stretches into infinity. You are a part of it – no more or less important than any other aspect; you have a connection with the stars, you are connected to every leaf of every tree, every root in the earth, every blade of grass, every grain of sand, every drop of rain and all the angels.

4. This huge being of Light is the Divine within you, your true, formless Higher Self – that part of you that sways to the music of the stars. This is your angel within, your Angel Light, who communicates wordlessly with celestial beings and has a part to play in the order of Universal Law. Your Higher Self knows exactly what your soul purpose is, and why you are here. All you have to do is connect with that higher wisdom, that part of you that knows the Divine and the angels, then trust and follow its guidance as you ask that you be shown what it is that you need to do. Stay in this sensation for a while, and then take some deep breaths to bring you back into your inner sacred space.

5. Take a moment now to pause, reflect and ask yourself: how can I connect more often in my daily life with this Divine part of me?

6. Holding your sacred space, explore the occasion when you felt drawn to the angels for the first time and note down any answers in your journal.

- What was happening to you and what were your feelings at the time?
- Who or what introduced you to the concept of a "Higher Self" and when?
- Can you recognize your inner beauty? Let's think of it as the angelic you, deep within your heart. When you are in touch with your "inner angel", how does this change your perception of the world around you? When did you first notice this?
- What are the angelic qualities you see in others, and when did you first notice them?
- What are your own angelic qualities, and when do you think you developed them?

The path of wisdom and illumination

When you have illuminating moments of awareness of something much greater than yourself, it can sometimes feel completely overwhelming. The glorious connection made with angels or the Divine – the bright lights you may see or feelings of warmth and support you may feel – often seems to fade just as rapidly and mysteriously as it appeared. This is the nature of the mystery. Mystics have sought and recorded that the search for a continuing sense of bliss is almost comparable to addiction. The highs are so exalted that real life can seem grey and boring by comparison. When we attain that magical sense of bliss, we cannot explain the sensations in adequate language. The sense of knowing, the bittersweet agony that can sometimes accompany the first exciting experience, and the moments after when many might begin to feel they have perhaps been wasting part of their life in a dull senseless existence. Even the psychotherapist Carl Jung, whose techniques were greatly influenced by his research into mystical practices,[4-5] noticed these extremes of emotion when he recorded his feelings after the uplifting mystical elation had faded: "This experience gave me a feeling of extreme poverty, but at the same time of great fullness."[6]

The other challenge to be aware of relates to the psychological changes that can occur as a result of a spiritual awakening. If the experience is gradual and you are careful to ground and protect your energies (see Step 1, Practice 3) then you are unlikely to suffer any detrimental effects. However, if the experience is a huge, life-changing event, such as a near-death experience or a dramatic vision, then you may need some guidance from a qualified psychotherapist to help you through it. These are called "spiritual emergencies" or "crises", and are more common than you might imagine. As a result, some people become disillusioned and leave their practice for many years; while others may become deluded and imagine that they are suddenly capable of healing the world, or creating a new world order or religious cult. It can also lead to evangelizing our new beliefs, which attract scepticism and even ridicule or rejection from our families and friends who don't quite understand the change.

Most of us stay somewhere in the middle. Just remember to always keep your feet on the ground, no matter how high your soul soars.

Trust your wisdom

Having tuned into your intuition with Gabriel in Step 1 (see page 39), working with Jophiel will encourage you to trust that internal wisdom more and more. You may start, for example, to notice that you are picking up on other people's vibrations.

Sometimes the energy feels great, other times it's not so good. You might feel that you no longer want to engage with loud or aggressive people because their energy is very prickly and different to your own. You may even find them toxic, their attitudes or opinions so prejudiced or negative that they are offensive to you.

You may sometimes feel like you're a little out of step, as though you're walking along with one foot on a different level. You are becoming more consciously aware and enjoying being in a positive space and so are more likely to notice and dislike being surrounded by anything negative. As a result, you may find that you have to make a decision to keep away from some of the people that you tolerated in the past. You might feel guilty, but try not to.

You may also find that you are more selective about which television channels and films you watch and the conversations you have. You are filling your life with positive energy, more fulfilling interests, creativity and wisdom, and you simply want to satisfy the craving for more of the "good stuff".

Use the following affirmation to help support you in trusting the wisdom that you have found in the Light of Archangel Jophiel. This will help you move away from anything that dulls your light or dampens your passion.

I trust my inner guidance, making positive choices for my wellbeing, knowing this also carries me towards the Light.

Using the practices you learned in Step 1 – the meditation with Gabriel (see page 35) and affirmation to strengthen your throat chakra (see page 47) – in addition to stepping into Jophiel's Light (see Practice 1, page 57) to enhance your wisdom and self-awareness will make it easier to express your own needs. This is an essential part of taking ownership of your life and integral to holistic personal and spiritual development.

DAILY PRAYER

Dear Archangel Jophiel,

Let your loving Light shine upon me now.

Shine your flame of illumination and enlighten my thoughts with your loving wisdom.

Guide my words that they reflect only truth and clarity.

Please enable my inner Light to shine that I may be a beacon of the Divine's Light in service to others.

Touch my heart and eyes that I may see the beauty of creation in everything.

I ask that you help me to reach my soul's potential that I may play my full part in co-creating this beautiful world.

Thank you.

Amen.

STEP 3

PRACTISE PROTECTION AND DISCERNMENT
LETTING GO OF FEAR AND CUTTING THE TIES THAT BIND WITH ARCHANGEL MICHAEL

"Nothing in life is to be feared, it is only to be understood. Now is the time to understand more, so that we may fear less."

Marie Curie

ANGEL ASSOCIATIONS

Attributes: Protection, Discernment, Truth, Strength, Letting Go

Colour: Keeper of the Blue Flame

Crystals: Sapphire, Lapis lazuli, Sodalite

Planetary influences: Sun

Day of the week: Sunday

Element: Fire

Ashram: High above Banff in the Canadian Rocky Mountains

After taking the bravest step of all: the first – in which we have been awakened and have learned the power of communication with Gabriel – by the second step we are buzzing with inspiration as we encounter aspects of our personal spiritual journey, creativity and receive a glimpse of fulfillment. Then along comes Michael to bring us right back down to earth by reminding us of the need of protection, teaching us discernment, and making us aware of staying within the boundaries of our own personal power.

In this step, you will learn how to call upon Michael's protective "sword and armour" and practise discernment in both your personal and spiritual life. As Michael's Light holds the vibration of sheer Divine power,[1] you many feel a real presence when you connect with Michael. He is also the most popular (and some say the only actual) Archangel.

Traditionally you may have already been taught to call on Michael for support and invoke him for protection in times of conflict. In this step, you'll learn that this power is available not just in extreme situations of violence or abuse, but in everyday life, for example when you're preparing to have a potentially difficult conversation with your boss, when dealing with annoying colleagues or a challenging family member. The practical exercises in this chapter will show you how to:

- Draw on Michael's magnificent, powerful blue Light to strengthen you, allowing you to stand up for yourself.
- Let go of any negative beliefs and ideas that are holding you back and choose helpful spiritual practices rather than those that may block your path.
- Use the image of Michael's sword to help you symbolically cut through mind chatter and self-limitations, find or follow a new direction, heal emotional wounds,

remind you of your inner strength and courage, and clear away distractions so that you can head forwards with passion and purpose.

- Practise discernment so that you are able to make wise choices that empower and enable you to speak and live your truth.
- Tune into Michael's Light to protect your aura, your home, family and environment.

Calling on Michael's strength and protection

There are many contemporary examples of people who have been "saved" by an angel. When I was researching for my previous book, *Gifts from Angels*, most of the stories sent to me were from people who had sensed or seen the colour blue around them at the time. They were left with an overwhelming sense of power and protection, leading them to believe they had been in the presence of Archangel Michael. But, as the nature of angelic beings is omnipresent, you don't need to "see" Michael in human form in order to step into his magnificent Light.

The powerful energy qualities that you will immediately sense when working with Michael are truth and discernment, strength and protection. This is because he is the Holy Warrior. In our human experience this can represent the best aspects of leadership. See him as a role model for living the best life you can, being truthful to your self and behaving honourably to others, in all situations. In order to do this you need to learn to practise discernment, Michael's other great teaching. In so doing you will learn to assess situations and people but not judge others or yourself harshly; you simply endeavour to live your truth and allow others to live theirs. Don't underestimate the great strength needed for this. You've already started the process in Step 1 by highlighting the link between truth and the throat chakra with Gabriel when we talked about communication (see Step 1, page 46). Here we give added power to that chakra and at the same time strengthen the solar plexus as we learn to build healthy boundaries and make wise choices in our relationships with others.

When you work with Michael's power in order to develop your own, you'll find that it will make you stronger and more resilient; it will be easier to live more "on purpose", and your Light will radiate more brightly.

PRACTICE 1
Drawing on the power of Archangel Michael for strength

Use the following guided meditation to step into Michael's Light to find the support you need to journey through Step 3, or whenever you feeling vulnerable or need to stand up for yourself in some way.

If you need to refresh your memory about using the guided meditations, see Tools for Your Journey (page 17).

1. Get comfortable and, if you choose, spend a few minutes breathing deeply before closing your eyes.
2. Continue to breathe yourself into a calm, grounded space and visualize a brilliant blue light before your eyes. Breathe this energy down through your body.
3. Call for Michael to wrap his cloak of blue around your shoulders and place his sword by your side and shield in front of you for protection by saying, "Archangel Michael, may I step into the presence of your Loving Light."

4. Visualize the power of the sword of Michael and lengthen your spine to be as straight and tall as the shining sword beside you.

5. Imagine the strength and brilliance of the metal as it shines like a bright light and know that you too are strong enough to deal with whatever comes your way. You will never be asked to face anything alone. The angels are always with you when you call. Trust that you are strong, honest and fair, always asking for the highest possible outcome, for the greatest good. All will be well.

6. Breathing slowly, deeply, deliberately, allow yourself to be back in the present moment. Bring yourself into your own space, your own room, and breathe normally. Feel your body: solid, present and fully grounded. Very slowly, when you're ready, open your eyes.

Letting go of self-limiting thoughts and beliefs

Working with angels is about strengthening your connection with the cosmic energy but also about growing as a person, becoming more compassionate, caring and acting from love. This happens more naturally when you spend time in conscious reflection, meditation or prayer and practise self-care (see also Step 1, page 51). When you start to treat yourself more kindly then your heart opens up not only to yourself but also to your family, friends and wider communities. This doesn't mean being a doormat; rather, becoming aware not only of your own needs but everyone else's too, and doing what you can to serve and treating others with loving-kindness – the way you would prefer to be treated yourself.

You cannot be of service, however, unless you consciously let go of any self-limiting beliefs or thoughts that prevent you from growing and moving forwards. For example, believing that you are controlled by a government, without which you are powerless, or the media, or any other organization or doctrine. Or thinking that the measure of success is material wealth, or that success in life is always based on gender. Or that you are unlucky in a particular aspect of life, that fortune hasn't been kind to you. You may also need to release invalid feelings of unworthiness, guilt and false expectations (of yourself and others) that dis-empower you, especially regarding your physical health, wellbeing or beauty.

You are learning to trust (from this moment on) that, actually, you are beautiful, unique and loved in your own way for who you are. The angelic realms see your Divine spark, the Light of your soul that shines through your eyes, not your physical body. It doesn't matter to them what you look like, the colour of your skin or the shade of your hair. They can detect physical disease and emotional disharmony, as that shows up as a change of colour and brightness in your aura, but your weight, height, gender and race are of no importance to them. Angels help, guide and love you no matter what, without conditions or hidden agenda.

> The greater service we may be to others, the wider our heart opens, the more angelic support we are able to receive, and the more Light we'll have to share.

Think of any self-limiting thoughts that creep into your mind regularly. All those reasons (and excuses) for not allowing yourself to be true to your purpose, your passion. The things in life that prevent you from doing what you would really like to do, like taking up a hobby, going on a retreat or signing up for an art or yoga class.

How many "can't do it", "can't go on my own" or "no one to go with", "impossible because..."-type reasons can you list from your own regular excuses?

- Do any of these reflect criticism from a partner or family member who doesn't share your spiritual beliefs, perhaps, which you heard and took on board for fear of rocking the boat?
- Do you have any outdated superstitions lurking in there too? If so, ask yourself: what are you basing these fears, restrictions or beliefs on? Is it time for you to safely let go of them now?
- Do you ever tell yourself that you are not clever enough, not qualified enough, too old, too young, or inadequate, etc.?
- Have you simply been telling yourself that you are only putting it off until you move house, earn more, find someone to do it with, find the right teacher, lose weight, and so on?

These "excuses" are absolutely real and practical in our heads, and might range from time constraints, childcare responsibilities, expectations from family and others to job restrictions, too many responsibilities, money worries, health issues, and so the list goes on. As we get older, many of us have demands from our children/grandchildren and elderly parents too. Then there are those little doubts that niggle from childhood: memories of being told that we were not good enough, no matter how hard we tried. Self-limiting beliefs are damaging and toxic and many allow these thoughts to plague them until they finally give up and decide they've missed the boat: "Oh well, its too late now!" No! It is never too late. This is only an imaginary timetable that they have allowed their fear to construct.

Let's face it, people really can, and do, have a change of career and become successful and happy in their fifties and sixties, then go on to run a marathon with a fit body developed in their seventies. There is absolutely no age limit.

Archangel Michael is always depicted in art wearing armour, representing the power of the Divine, and very often a red robe or red lining to his cloak, signifying his role as a Seraph (belonging to the highest order of celestial beings). He carries the great silver sword of righteousness, and this represents an etheric power, which we may call upon to use in practical ways, such as in meditative exercises, to protect, empower and support our growth. Use the following self-enquiry exercise to think about what could be standing between you and living your life more purposefully.

PRACTICE 2
Renewing self-confidence and fulfilling your dreams

1. Grab your journal and write a wish list of everything you would do if you could (that is, if you stopped living to an imaginary timetable or making excuses), whether it's dying your hair red, climbing a mountain or learning how to paint.
2. Be really honest and make a list of the reasons for NOT doing these things that would make your soul sing – anything, whether real or imagined, you have used to persuade yourself that you were not "fit for purpose".

3. Close your eyes and ask Archangel Michael to empower you to find the determination to succeed in fulfilling your dreams. Ask for help in bringing the right people into your life to support you.

4. Now rearrange your wish list, putting those things that are clearly "do-able", like getting more exercise, reading that book you ordered, changing your hairstyle, practising yoga, learning the basics of a new language or losing weight, at the top, gradually working your way down to the things that would realistically be a little more challenging to organise (like climbing Mount Everest or winning gold at the Olympics).

5. Next, look at the logistics of what you would need to do to be able to accomplish the most easily accessible wish, the one at the top of your list. Can you do it? Yes, you can.

6. Write out the affirmation *"I believe in myself and am able to do this now"* on a piece of paper and put it somewhere you will see it. Make sure you say it at the beginning of every day.

7. Repeat the affirmation in sets of three, as often as you can, and especially if and when doubt creeps in.

8. The more you do and the greater your self-belief, the more accessible your list will become. Your renewed confidence and high energy may soon attract helpful friends who make these achievements even more accessible.

Michael's sword: overcoming the blocks that hold you back

As well as supporting your physical and spiritual growth, Michael can also be called upon for emotional and psychic protection.

You can ask for the energy of Michael to give you physical protection when you are travelling, simply by asking, "Archangel Michael, protect me please", and imagining a blue light of protection surrounding you, your companions and your vehicle. You might also like to use the following affirmation:

> *I stand in my power knowing protective Angel Light safely surrounds me.*

Michael's sword is a wonderful symbolic tool for cutting away all the old negative thinking and clearing the way for new opportunities and possibilities. For example, you might like to take a moment to think of ways you could use a sword in real life, if all your restrictions were presented to you as real objects rather than abstract thoughts. What beliefs and thoughts would you cut away? If all your "ties" were ropes around your ankles, would you use the sword to cut through and release them? If you were in a hot air balloon but grounded due to the weight of sand bags (your own limitations) around the sides, would you cut them free so you could rise up? If all your baggage was being dragged behind you in a fishing net tied to your waist, would you cut through it and set yourself free?

If you feel ready to let go of some of the patterns that have developed into ties and restrictions that hold you back – and some of these may well feel like heavy ropes or chains around you – then here is a powerful meditation to try.

PRACTICE 3
Meditation for cutting unwanted ties

This practice is designed to enhance your soul connection with Michael's Light and help you cut any unhelpful ties that are holding you back.

Before starting the meditation, take a moment to bring to mind anything that is preventing you from pursuing a particular goal. This might be someone from the past (or present) whose voice of authority or negativity takes your power away and inhibits your progress. Or it could be your own inner "monkey-mind" chatterbox. It might be an ongoing issue with someone you know, or a habit, addiction or behaviour pattern that you know is self-limiting or restricts you in some way. Once you know your intention, you are ready to cut one self-limiting belief at a time.

You can also listen to this exercise as a meditation download at www.AngelLight.co.uk/sevensteps.

1. Light a candle and then invite your guardian angel and the presence of Archangel Michael into your sacred space, by saying, "Archangel Michael, may I step into the presence of your Loving Light."
2. Get yourself into a comfortable sitting position, close your eyes and breathe deeply. Allow your body to let go of all tensions with every exhalation.
3. Visualize a beautiful, vibrant, blue light surrounding you and breathe it in with every breath.
4. Now see the light forming into a continuously moving beam flowing around and in front of you, creating a horizontal figure-of-eight with you in one half of it.

5. As the light continues to flow, imagine the issue as an unwanted gift, or imagine the challenging person and place it, or invite them, into the other half of the bright blue figure-of-eight. (If it is difficult or painful for you to imagine a person so close to you then create a symbol for them instead.)

6. Ask Archangel Michael and the angels to help you in this process of cutting the ties that bind you. Do this aloud if you can, or very clearly in your mind.

7. Call your own guardian angel to stand with you in your side of the eight, and an angel of Michael in the other.

8. Now, sensing the radiance and power of Archangel Michael, visualize his great silver sword like a laser beam cutting through the figure of eight and separating it into two circles.

9. As you stand in your safe blue circle of Angel Light, watch in your mind's eye as Michael's angel lovingly takes away the other circle. Keep watching in your mind's eye as it moves slowly into the light. Think only positive thoughts of gratitude and love.

10. Thank Michael from your heart and sit in the peace and calm for a while.

11. Breathing slowly, deeply, deliberately, allow yourself to be back in the present moment. Bring yourself into your own space, your own room, and breathe normally. Feel your body: solid, present and fully grounded. Very slowly, when you're ready, open your eyes.

Michael's etheric sword can also be used to point in a new direction, as a warrior would point the way ahead, simply by bringing to mind the direction in which you want to head. Close your eyes and visualize Michael's sword pointing the way.

The sharp point of the sword can also be used to cut away an emotional wound. Ask Michael to "touch" the pain and dissolve any feelings of being "hurt". In conflict, a soldier might also point a sword at the throat in order to extract the truth from a villain or conniving rebel. We can think of this as a metaphor of Archangel Michael pointing his sword to our own throat chakra (the centre of our communication and will), in a firm but very non-threatening way, simply reminding us to reveal our truth; to be authentic to our true self.

The ruling monarch would also use a sword to commend and reward a valiant knight for his bravery and service to the realm. A beautiful decorative sword would be given as a highly valued gift to brave knights at the fulfilment of their training, so using a sword in your visualizations does not mean it is always about battle – it can serve to remind us of our achievements too.

Place an image of Archangel Michael with his sword on your altar and allow it to remind you how Michael's Light can help you:

- Cut through mind chatter and distractions.
- Find or follow a new direction.
- Heal an emotional wound.
- Remind you of your strength and courage.
- Clear away distractions and point in a new direction, as a warrior might do.

Discernment

When we reach a point of awareness where we are mindful of the need to change, we may decide that we can no longer tolerate those things that cause us anxiety or pain: something inside our heart senses the need to let them go. This sharpens a particular kind of emotional response and helps us to change direction away from the offending situation. In spiritual terms, we call it "discernment" – the ability to tell the difference between what is truth and error, honesty and deception, right and wrong. It is the process we use to make wise decisions.

Spiritual discernment has a deeper layer, and so to the above we add the ability to be able to make careful distinctions between authentic and false spiritual teachings, good and bad practice, positive and negative energies. Spiritual discernment is fundamental not only for deciding what is true, but for building wisdom. Having looked at how to work on spiritual wisdom lovingly in Step 2, here we can now build it firmly into a spiritual practice to help us make the right choices.

When something happens in life that requires a decision based on various choices, trust that your own soul knows best. So, ask yourself: how does it make you feel? If you get a surge of energy that makes you want to punch the air, or rush off and hop and skip, then take that option as a resounding "Yes". If the sensation is either fear in the pit of your stomach or a "blanch" reaction, you know it is a definite "no". You can also call in Michael to help you discern the truth by taking a moment to centre yourself, visualizing a blue light and calling his name, while also feeling into your own body for a strong reaction.

Dowsing for answers

You can also use a dowsing crystal pendulum or favourite necklace to swing over the question, tuning into your own energy to show you a "yes" or a "no".

Simply hold the chain steady, about 10cm (4in) above the pendant, then mentally ask for a clear sign for "yes". The pendant will then start to move – take the movement, whether it swings backwards and forwards or goes around in circles, as "yes". Then ask for a clear "no". The movement will be different; even if, for example, the pendant is still moving in circles, they might now be going in the opposite direction. Take whatever movement it makes as the sign for "no". Test it by asking: "Am I [your own name]?", then "Am I [a friend's name]?" This will confirm the movements for you.

Tuning into Michael's protective energy

There is no doubt that bringing Michael's Light into daily life helps guide us towards what is true and shields us from deceit.

Truth, however, can be both subjective, in that it holds and reflects our personal sense of what is right or wrong, and objective, as it reflects what is commonly held as true on a universal scale. So, for instance, certain dogmatic religious beliefs may be held passionately as truth by one community but may not be held by a majority worldview. I may believe that if I recite certain mantras or chants that I will gain merit with Buddha, or that Jesus died to save my sins, if that is my religious belief. But if I am not a Buddhist or a Christian, it will not be my truth.

If we look back in history for an example of a "universal" truth, it was once widely believed that the world was flat. Of course, we now know that is not the case. When I was at school I was told that the smallest particle was an atom. We now know that isn't true either. So some truths are personal and true only for us, and some things are possibly untrue but held as a truth by a whole group.

95

Your truth, therefore, will reflect and contain ideas relative to your age, family dynamic, environment, education, culture, ancestry, social group, race, religion, upbringing, gender and nationality. This also is true of those who impart their truths to you: your parents, carers and teachers. Your truth, just like the effects of the life you have led, can often show in your facial expressions without you even knowing. If you are emotionally literate and aware of these giveaway signs in your own demeanour, you can learn to read them in other people too. Noticing tone of voice and other signs in body language and behaviour helps you in very practical ways to discern the truth. For example, human psychology studies into body language have shown that shuffling can indicate embarrassment and looking away suggests that the person is avoiding the truth.

At times people will project their perspective onto someone else, often unwittingly. If this has happened to you it can be awkward at best and excruciatingly painful at worst. When this projection is carried out maliciously, for example if people are being spiteful and causing trouble behind your back, this is often the basis of what's commonly called a "psychic attack".

Tuning into the protective energy of the Archangel Michael and asking for Divine protection definitely helps us to combat these painful experiences and we can do this by seeing and feeling into our aura[2] with our five senses.

When we are happy, positive and balanced, our own auric field enlarges and spreads out, while negative or toxic ideas that are harmful to us, or our health, cause it to reverse and shrink into our physical body. We can demonstrate this without the use of any equipment. Quite simply, we'll know if we don't like someone, or they have a very negative disposition, because we'll automatically back away – as though they have invaded our space. They have. Very often its because we don't have a compatible vibration. Think of some of the phrases we use in everyday speech: "That person has a lovely energy" (when we enjoy being their company) or "We are not on the same wavelength" (if we find the conversation in some way disagreeable or awkward).

When we are bombarded by negativity, it actually weakens our aura. There are other ways, though, that we can cause damage our own energy levels, which in turn reflects in our aura. Some are very obvious, like looking after a sick person for a long time, which can be physically and emotionally draining. Dealing with the demands of small children, however pleasurable, can create mental exhaustion, and working in a constantly demanding and pressurized atmosphere can create stress, which as we know leads to long-term damage on many levels.

All these stresses cause holes and cracks to appear in our aura. At this point other people – especially those we might call "Energy Vampires" – can drain our energy too, whether intentionally because they want some of ours, or unintentionally just by being what we call "needy". This is where, if we don't take care, the negativity can creep in and damage our own health. A damaged aura leads to even more fatigue and a lowered mental capacity to cope with everyday life because it is leaking our energy. At this point if we don't stop it progressing, depression and other forms of subtle and serious emotional and mental illness can manifest.

Ways to protect your aura

There are a few simple but effective methods that can help you bring conscious protection into your daily routine:

1: Protect your chakras

The chakra that most frequently leaks energy when you are unprotected is the solar plexus. One of the easiest ways to protect this chakra is simply to gently cross your arms in front of your body when speaking to anyone that you feel is sapping your energy. You can also protect all your chakras as preparation for healing or spiritual work by imagining each of your seven chakras as a spinning open portal on your body. Now visualize each one in turn, starting at the root and working right up to the crown. Filling each chakra with Angel Light, draw an equal-sided cross surrounded by a ring at each point with your finger in the air in front of you. In your mind you can do this symbolic ritual to protect each chakra at the back, too (see also Tools for Your Journey, page 27).

When I first trained in angelic healing, I was told to "close and protect" all my chakras, in front of me and behind me (the chakras operate from both directions). Of course I did as I was instructed. But as I explored my spiritual impulse I found that the idea of "closing down" all my chakras didn't sit comfortably with me at all. I now prefer to keep my heart open as wide as possible. That way I can share love, even though just like everyone else I can sometimes feel the hurt of others a little too much, being an empath. I also prefer to open my third eye whenever I'm working, and my crown whenever I wish to connect with the Divine and the angelic realms as much as possible too. I protect all my chakras by calling in Michael's protective Light around my whole aura. This then allows the flow of inspiration to and from the Divine. However, closing down the chakras is very important at the early stages in your journey and can help

protect your energy. As you grow in confidence you may prefer to
keep them more open as I often do.

2: Create a protective circle of Divine Light

Every morning, just as you get out of bed, imagine that you are stepping straight into a circle of bright gold or white light. Sit on the edge of the bed and swing your feet onto the floor. Bending over, touch your toes in the "circle of light". As you stand up, draw it up and around you and over your head with your hands, visualizing the light enfolding you. As if you are doing a first-thing-in-the-morning stretch, swing your arms and stretch out your hands around you, bringing all the light into your aura. As you stretch your arms above your head, meet your hands together and visualize that you are encased in a beautiful capsule of golden or white light. Finally, simply say to yourself: "I am protected."

The beauty of this practice is that it not only invokes Michael's strength but also gives you a moment to intentionally stretch your body and lengthen your spine, which is both an act of self-care and means you start the day walking tall.

3: Shower away negativity

As part of your morning shower and self-care routine, you can consciously cleanse your aura of any negativity under the running water. Call upon the angels, especially the angel of the element of water, Archangel Raphael in Step 4 (see Practice 4, page 129), to cleanse and purify your auric energy as you shower. As you get out of the shower and wrap a towel around you, imagine that you are being enfolded in a beautiful soft and protective light.

4: Bless and protect your home

Before you leave home, bless it. Give thanks for all the good things in your home and as you close the door visualize filling it with love and light. You might like to say: "I bless my home with loving light, in gratitude for the comfort and safety it provides for me. I ask Archangel Michael to surround it with loving Light and protection. Thank you."

As you get into your car, on the bus, or whatever method of transport you take, visualize the blue Light of Michael surrounding your entire home and holding the sacred energy in place until you return.

5: Bless ahead

Bless your day ahead, all those you work with and those you will meet during the day. Bless the outcome of every situation in advance, asking for and expecting the best for all concerned.

You might like to say: "I bless the day before me, all those I will meet. I ask that all challenges I may encounter be blessed, and that all will result in the best possible outcome for the highest good for all concerned. Thank you."

6: Use crystals and gems

Choose jewellery made from crystals or a particular gemstone with symbolic or emotional significance to you. We know that deeply coloured stones, such as rubies, sapphires and amethysts, offer protection. Diamonds are very powerful and have the benefit of containing all the colours of the spectrum when held in the light. A gold or crystal bracelet on each wrist and a pendant hanging at heart level also offer energy protection against negative vibrations. You might also find it helpful to place a piece of lapis lazuli, amethyst, clear quartz (to clear the energy) or blue selenite (to strengthen your connection with the angelic realms) – the crystals associated with Michael – on your desk at work to remind you of his protective power. When you feel overwhelmed by your inbox or to-do list, touch your crystal. Breathe deeply and remind yourself that Divine support is always there when you ask for it. You may also like to use the following affirmation:

I calmly engage with the living energy of these crystals to add light and strength to my aura. As I stand within my own power I know that I am protected and all is well.

7: Call upon the powerful Archangel Michael

Last but certainly not least, call upon the power of Archangel Michael to surround you with his Divine Light. You can imagine a beautiful blue light shining on and around you. If you are feeling particularly vulnerable or have an especially challenging or potentially confrontational meeting ahead, you can ask that his sacred sword and armour protect you. You might say something as simple as: "Archangel Michael, protect me please."

There are lots of other lovely ways to bring protection into your daily life too, such as crystals, candles, bells, sprays, incense, smudge sticks and essences. Use crystals to clear the energy in your home and candles to invite in the light. Sprays and essences can clear and lift the energy in the room. For example, I use essences that have been intuitively channelled for my use made from flower and crystal distillations or oils, which contain particular spiritual attributes such as rose for love and sandalwood for lifting the mood. Incense clears and cleanses the room of any stale energy and adds its own warming sacred aroma to the atmosphere.

TAKE CARE

Take care not to become dependant on any of the above rituals to protect your aura, or develop these suggestions into a superstition. Remember: you will not suddenly be unprotected if you don't use one or all of them.

Protecting yourself with positivity

While we have looked at the effect that negative energies can have on us and how to protect yourself, remember it's important not to talk yourself into fear in the process. The Earth has a natural polarity and positive and negative charges are naturally present everywhere. We too have positive and negative energies all around us in different forms: underground water, geopathic stress, electronic equipment, overhead wires, mobile phone transmitters and vehicle emissions have all been found to cause fatigue. But here our focus should not be on fear, rather awareness of anything that may dim our Light so that we can avoid it and consciously make the decision to shine even brighter.

As you gather momentum on this seven-step journey, Michael's powerful attributes of protection and discernment contribute valuable and practical spiritual tools which you can now use whenever you need to.

DAILY PRAYER

Dear Archangel Michael,

I call upon the mighty I AM presence, and the Sacred Sword of Truth.

Please help me to release all self-limiting thoughts and false expectations I have of myself and others. Teach me the use of loving balance of power in all relationships.

Grant me the gift of discernment that I may recognize my true path.

And guide me in realizing my highest spiritual potential, shining my Divine Light in honesty and truth.

Thank you.

Amen.

STEP 4

BECOME WHOLE
DISCOVERING SELF-HEALING
WITH ARCHANGEL RAPHAEL

"The wound is the place where the light enters you."

Jalaluddin Rumi

ANGEL ASSOCIATIONS

Attributes: Healing, Scientific Discovery, Medicine,
   Consecration, Wholeness
Colour: Keeper of the Emerald-green Flame
Crystals: Emerald, Peridot, Fuchsite, Jade, Green
   Moldavite
Planetary influence: Mercury
Day of the week: Thursday
Element: Water
Ashram: Above Fatima in Portugal

In the previous step, working with Archangel Michael's Light reminds us of the necessities of learning and practising the art of discernment. He empowers and protects our energies from all angles, and enables us to let go of limiting beliefs that don't serve us.

Now at last we are ready to embark on a great healing adventure with Archangel Raphael, the Divine's great healer and an amazing angelic force for good. *Rapha* in Hebrew means "doctor" or "healer", and "El" means "shining one". When we understand the depth and power of Raphael's Light, we realize we can also heal any sense of lacking or insufficiency, too, because Raphael helps us to create a sense of gratitude and abundance.

Raphael is the third of the "big four" Archangels, along with Michael, Gabriel and Uriel, and his energy is linked to the heart chakra. As I mentioned earlier, when we talked about turning ordinary places into sacred spaces (see Tools for Your Journey, page 23), Raphael is the Angel of Consecration. By invoking his high vibrational healing light you can clear stale, negative or even malevolent energy from areas where you wish to create a sacred space or simply buildings that just don't feel right. This is particularly important before setting out on your healing journey.

Stepping into Raphael's Light, you will find that you become more aware and tuned into your own "body talk". You'll become more open to eliminating emotional toxins and gain more insight into how your thoughts can make you sick. You will also learn deep healing techniques so that you are ready to step fully into a loving embrace with your purpose in the final three steps. In preparation, with the over-lighting guidance of Archangel Raphael, the practical exercises in this chapter show you how to:

- Heal stress, anxiety or toxic/negative thoughts and memories that are suppressing your sense of wellbeing and potentially resulting in poor health.
- Forgive yourself and others, even if you still feel aggrieved or angry. By dissolving these harmful

emotions you can begin healing the emotional pain held in your body.

- Connect more deeply with your chakra energy, and bring healing to all parts of your life, to support the deeper healing that this step will bring.
- Create sacred space in your home or anywhere you work.
- Discover some of the secrets of soothing relationships.

Healing emotional wounds

Linked strongly to your heart chakra and emotions, Raphael's Light can help you heal deeper emotional wounds, such as those caused by human relationships. For example, if you've ever had a row with your lover or partner – the kind of argument that echoes in your head so long you don't know which way to turn – you'll know that it can leave you feeling weak or sick for days.

Very few of us have escaped the pain that a rift within a relationship can cause. Of course, we may fall out with friends or family, and experience differences of opinion with work colleagues, which can leave us feeling miserable... but the greatest pain and deepest wounds are usually due to our closest "loving" relationships. Not only divorce but also continual bickering, or bullying, means that many lovely people are carrying the scars of a failed or toxic relationship. Sometimes the pain is fresh and raw, but in many cases the rift still causes hurt after decades. It is so important to be able to heal our emotional wounds before they become too deep.

Evidence shows that other cells within our amazing human body have a memory of their own, not just within the brain, and will hold onto the pain in certain areas, particularly the joints or heart and chest area. This weakens us, often to the point of debilitating physical discomfort and chronic "dis-ease".

Sibling rifts or even major problems within our families that we might label "dysfunctional" can also be seen with a new perspective, worked out, and differences soothed with Raphael's healing energy. Unfortunately, it isn't quite as simple as saying, "Angels, take this all away and make it better please." We still have to commit to regular spiritual practice of prayer, meditation and self-reflection. We need to accept that we too have a role to play in the conflict. But incredible changes can occur when love and healing, rather than negativity and rancour, are the focus.

Everything starts in our thoughts, our consciousness, and so we can work with Raphael's light to help reverse the degeneration in our cells, our thoughts and our relationships.

The following three-part guided meditation with Archangel Raphael can start the process of healing.

PRACTICE 1, PART I
Cellular healing with Raphael

In the first part of this guided meditation, you'll call upon the powerful green healing Light of Archangel Raphael to deal with stress, anxiety and any toxic/negative thoughts that are causing you pain or poor health.

If you need to refresh your memory about using the guided meditations, see Tools for Your Journey (page 17), or, you can listen to or download a meditation with Raphael here: www.AngelLight.co.uk/sevensteps.

1. Get comfortable and, if you choose, spend a few minutes breathing deeply in the light of your candle before closing your eyes.

2. Continue breathing slowly and consciously, taking the breath down into your abdomen and releasing away any tension with every exhalation. When you are ready, call upon the energy of Archangel Raphael, three times, aloud if possible (remember that the number three has a powerful mystical property which, when used as a mantra, magnifies the intention of your prayer or request): "Archangel Raphael, may I step into the power of your beneficent healing Light."

3. Now imagine a beautiful green light surrounding you and filling your whole body from head to toe with a balancing and peaceful healing light.

4. Ask the powerful energy of Archangel Raphael to cleanse any toxic thoughts or memories that are causing you pain.

5. Imagine the green light calming your mind as you breathe it in for a few moments, or as long as you like, balancing your energies and repairing your cells.

6. Say the following affirmation to yourself three times, and then as often as you like, always in sets of three: "*Every cell in my being works in perfect harmony.*"

7. Breathing slowly, deeply, deliberately, allow yourself to be back in the present moment. Bring yourself into your own space, your own room, and breathe normally. Feel your body: solid, present and fully grounded. Very slowly, when you're ready, open your eyes.

Healing blame and guilt

One of the greatest and most compassionate gifts we can offer ourselves is to cease fault-finding or harshly judging and condemning ourselves (and other people for that matter). The greatest healing we can experience comes with the act of forgiveness because when we carry blame, guilt or shame we hurt. If we blame others and pile guilt onto them, we are only hurting them, which in return hurts us more. Forgiveness will be a key theme in the following two steps on our journey together with the Archangels, as we move towards love and living more in line with a whole and loving purpose.

PRACTICE 1, PART II
Healing self-blame and judgement with Raphael

In the second part of this guided meditation, you call on Raphael to help you heal any harmful emotions that are due to a painful relationship. It can be any relationship, not necessarily with a lover. You need to be ready to do this, as it is a very powerful sacred ritual, so if it feels too challenging you may decide to return to it at a later date.

Remember that at this stage you can also draw on earlier light energy from the other Archangels you have already worked with at previous steps. You are gathering tools for use along your journey and they can all be used to add power to any exercise. (This exercise will heal on many levels but if you have been the victim of severe mental or physical abuse, I encourage you to seek professional therapy or counselling as well.)

1. Begin by breathing slowly and consciously, taking the breath down into your abdomen and releasing away any tension with every exhalation.

2. Call Archangel Raphael three times and ask that his powerful green light surrounds you for this exercise.
3. Picture the person or partner (with whom you have the issue) as happy and well.
4. Now picture in your mind's eye a whole circle of angels surrounding that person. With Archangel Raphael by your side, you enter the circle and stand facing the person.
5. In this safe and sacred space, imagine looking into their eyes and say: "I truly forgive you for any pain you have caused me, whether intentionally or unintentionally... I ask you to forgive me too for any pain I might have also caused you, whether intentionally or unintentionally."
6. Open yourself to feel the love of all the angels in the circle as both of you receive a healing blessing from Archangel Raphael.
7. Breathing slowly, deeply, deliberately, allow yourself to be back in the present moment. Bring yourself into your own space, your own room, and breathe normally. Feel your body: solid, present and fully grounded. Very slowly, when you're ready, open your eyes.

There are three elements to compassion: love, kindness and patience. It is often easy to be loving, kind and patient with someone else but much more difficult to apply these qualities to ourselves.

Angels work only at the level of absolute pure love and the Light and energy of Archangel Raphael promotes deep healing with compassion by reminding us how unique, beautiful and loved all of us really are.

PRACTICE 1, PART III
Stepping into Compassion

In the final part of this practice, Archangel Raphael encourages you to step into the energy of compassion for yourself, and share that feeling with others, even those who have hurt you.

1. Begin by breathing slowly and consciously, taking the breath down into your abdomen and releasing away any tension with every exhalation.
2. Close your eyes for a moment and imagine you can see a tiny ball of light forming behind your eyes. Watch as it grows, becoming brighter and brighter, reminding you that this is the light of your own higher consciousness, your soul, your Divine Light. Give this ball of light your love and admiration, just as you would any other thing of great beauty and value.
3. Now imagine the other person that has hurt you in some way, with a similar beautiful light shining from within.
4. Say in your head, or out loud if you prefer: "The Divine Light within me acknowledges and loves the Divine Light within you." By moving the focus to each other's Divine Light, you can have compassion for yourself and your partner without reintroducing negativity into the situation.
5. Breathing slowly, deeply, deliberately, allow yourself to be back in the present moment. Bring yourself into your own space, your own room, and breathe normally. Feel your body: solid, present and fully grounded. Very slowly, when you're ready, open your eyes.
6. Give yourself a hug!

Healing your mind: energy follows thought

You may already be aware of the work of Deepak Chopra, Louise Hay, William Bloom, Caroline Myss, Dr Wayne Dyer, Sandy Stevenson and other spiritual writers who have penned their ideas of self-healing through awareness and a heightened understanding of how the power of thoughts and emotions affect the body. There are two fundamental concepts:

1. Your body is a mirror of your life.
2. You are an energy being.

I cannot emphasize enough how important it is to become fully aware that everything you think and feel creates who you are physically – every line etched on your face, every ache and pain. Energy follows thought, thought creates words and action, therefore everything that happens in your life, and within your body, starts within your consciousness and reflects your personal energy. This is not just who you are and how you are seen by others, it is how you experience your "being". Your experience of "being" is energy that isn't just in your brain but in every cell of your body, and held in the light surrounding your body: your auric field. How you communicate with your body through your consciousness affects every organ and every tissue.

We know that stress affects our health, as study after study names it as a contributing factor in many serious diseases, including heart disease, type-2 diabetes and cancer.[1] We can see it most clearly demonstrated in post-traumatic stress disorder (PTSD).[2] But throughout childhood, adolescence and adulthood, as you decide what to believe, what to accept or reject, some decisions leave you with residual stress, while stress and burnout due to overwork or overwhelm are now as a much a norm in our society as the common cold.

The way you cope with stress, your mental attitude and how your consciousness is communicated throughout the body will, needless to say, affect you in the moment, but also have a lasting effect on your future health and wellbeing.

How we each deal with emotional stress depends on the understanding that:

Energy follows thought.
Energy can be felt.
Energy can be changed before it affects the physical body.
We create our reality.

These statements might seem overly simplistic. Nevertheless, knowing something and taking action to change it are often two different things. For a long time we have known that stress is carried and held in the body. Science proves this.[3] Just as certain areas of the body carry memories in the cells, such as heartache and grief in the chest and lungs, anger in the solar plexus (liver and gallbladder), and bitterness and resentment in the joints, we also know that reducing stress heals the body.

You may already have an understanding how energy life force flows through the body. Perhaps you have experienced the effect of Chinese acupuncture on the meridian energy lines throughout the body or are familiar with the Indian chakra system. In traditional Chinese medicine, the flow of energy is called "chi"; in Indian: "prana". These ancient systems were brought to us from the Eastern philosophies at the turn of the 20th century but have become better known in the last 20–30 years with the rise in popularity of yoga, Reiki, tai chi, meditation and mindfulness.

This is one way of understanding how the energy circulates through the body and governs important physical, emotional and mental wellbeing. I have already mentioned these vital energy centres, called chakras, (see Tools for Your Journey, page 27), but let's go into them in more depth with a view of understanding how they can help us heal stress.

Chakras: portals to healing

Each of the chakras is a cone-shaped vortex of spinning energy from the front and back of the body. Each spins at a different speed, holds a different vibrational frequency, and relates not only to the area of the body in which it is situated, but the various ages of development and sacred passages through life.

The chakras are not limited to those described earlier in the book (see Tools for Your Journey, page 27). We also have chakra points at the tips of our fingers, along the soles of our feet, and several others reaching upwards above our crown. In the Seven Steps, we mainly focus on the primary chakras but by understanding the effect of all the chakras you'll find a level of empowerment and vitality that enables you to establish a balanced life. Once you come to understand your energy system, you will be able to identify any deficiencies you may have, heal them and enjoy a more complete, fulfilling life.

Turn to the table in the Appendix and you'll see that each chakra is associated with the organs, limbs, muscles, etc. within that particular area of the body, and how they can affect your health if they are either blocked or low in energy. You will also be able to work out where the emotional blockages are situated in relation to the areas of discomfort within your own body. The function of each chakra has several emotional and behavioural characteristics, too. This is probably most obvious when you look at the function of the heart chakra, but knowing the others is more than useful – especially if you are to understand how energy flows throughout your whole body.

PRACTICE 2
Connecting more deeply to your body

Start by using Practice 1 in Step 1 (see page 35). Visualize your entire body and illuminate all parts of it, starting from your toes. Feel deeply for any discomfort. Ask yourself what you think this might be telling you.

Then look at the table in the Appendix (see page 220).

- Can you relate any of this information to any problems you may have had in the past?
- As you observe any tension in your body now, do you recognise the development of that tension through the years?

Now, having done the "body scanning" exercise above, revisit the timeline that you created in Step 1 (see Practice 4, page 48). This time – perhaps in a different colour – mark your seven-year intervals with any illnesses or health challenges you may have had in the relevant periods along the timeline, right up to the present moment. Also mark at the starting point anything you know of that affected your mother during her pregnancy, or at your birth.

Reflect on your memories for each period of development in seven-year cycles to see if you can find any cellular memory pattern you may be carrying which is no longer appropriate for you (and, indeed, may even be holding back your spiritual, emotional and physical development).

Taking your time, reflect deeply on each question and be totally honest with yourself. Again, please be kind to yourself. There are no "right" or "wrong" answers. This is for you to assess, without judgement, which (if any) areas of your energy system require healing or some clearing of inappropriate cellular memories.

Answer the following questions with one of these words, whichever feels the most appropriate to you: always, sometimes, seldom, never. You can add the answers here or in your journal if you prefer.

1. Root chakra

1. Do you allow yourself to "stop and smell the roses"?
2. Do you take time to enjoy and connect with nature, in parks, gardens, the countryside, by the sea?
3. Does it feel good to go barefoot (on the sand, carpet, grass)?
4. Are you happy in your work?
5. Is there structure in your life?
6. Would you describe yourself as a patient person?
7. If you feel you are running round in circles, getting nowhere, are you able to stop, evaluate and change the situation straight away?
8. If you have ever felt a "victim" of circumstance or other people's choices, were you able to remain positive and focused?

2. Sacral chakra

1. Would you say that you enjoy life?

2. Do you enjoy regular physical exercise such as walking?
3. Do you make time to enjoy personal physical pampering such as massage, and take plenty of breaks and holidays?
4. Is sex an important, pleasurable and fulfilling part of your life (or has been when you were in a relationship)?
5. Do you eat consciously with foods that nourish and sustain your health?
6. Are you able to say no to things and people who are not good for you, even toxic?
7. Do you take responsibility for how happy you feel?
8. Do you recognize and acknowledge peace, love, kindness, abundance and beauty in your life?

3. Solar plexus chakra

1. Do you feel free to choose in every situation?
2. Do you accept freedom of choice is essential to your development?
3. Are you willing to exert your own power if you feel wronged?
4. Are you confident in your ability to communicate your needs?
5. Are you confident in your life skills?
6. Do you respect yourself for having done a good job so far, honouring your achievements?
7. Do you honour your position within your family and amongst your friends, shining your Light even when you feel different?
8. Can you complete a task through to its conclusion?

4. Heart chakra

1. Do you experience joy in your life through people and nature?
2. Do you create peace in your professional and home life?
3. Do you feel love for yourself?
4. Are you able to offer love to others unconditionally?
5. Are you able to forgive those who may have hurt you?
6. Are you able to apologize readily, and to forgive yourself?
7. Do you see those around you as equals?
8. Do you love sharing things you care about?

5. Throat chakra

1. Do you say what you really feel?
2. Are you able to stay silent when appropriate?
3. Are you open, clear and honest in your communication?
4. Can you be honest with yourself even when confronted or opposed?
5. Can you tell when someone is lying or deceiving you?
6. Are you dependable? Do you actually do what you say you are going to do?
7. Do you tune into and listen to your body, mind and spirit to find your truth?
8. Do you feel you have a strong willpower to make any changes required?

6. Third Eye/Brow chakra

1. Can you trust what your intuition tells you about people or places?

2. Can you use your intuition to sense what is best for you, rather than the powerful influence of, say, psychics, gurus or clairvoyants?
3. Can you tell the difference between knowledge and wisdom?
4. Can you look back and acknowledge the wisdom you have gained?
5. Can you discern manipulation and those who are on your side?
6. Can you visualize easily?
7. Do you notice when you are giving to others at the expense of your own happiness, and change things?
8. Do you give yourself time for reading and enjoying uplifting, inspirational books?

7. Crown chakra

1. Do you see the beauty in everything around you, creating peace and love where possible?
2. Do you allow your own inner beauty to shine?
3. Are you able to open your awareness to a higher power?
4. Can you release any ideas of limitation and fulfil your potential?
5. Do you put challenges and difficulties into a spiritual context?
6. Do you feel you are loved, cherished and valued by the Divine/Universe?
7. Do you connect with the wonder of life?
8. Do you regularly experience a sense of bliss?

Once you have answered the questions, give yourself points depending on whether you answered always (4 points), sometimes (3), seldom (2) or never (0).

Now add up the points for each section. You will see straight away by its lower score which area you need to work harder on. (This is a super exercise to do with a friend, then discuss your scores.)

Strengthening the weaker chakras includes calling in Archangel Raphael for healing and balance in the following visualization (you can include each of the appropriate Archangels for each chakra too if you wish). Strengthen them by using the affirmations, and meditating on the colours of the chakras (imagine yourself floating through a rainbow, for example), but, most importantly, by valuing and honouring yourself, being mindful of your self-talk and being aware of sources of stress in your life.

PRACTICE 3
Self-healing with Raphael

Use the following guided meditation to step into Raphael's Light and bring healing to all parts of your life.

If you need to refresh your memory about using the guided meditations, see Tools for Your Journey (page 17), or, if you prefer to listen to it as a meditation download, go to: www.AngelLight.co.uk/sevensteps.

1. Get comfortable and, if you choose, spend a few minutes breathing deeply before closing your eyes.

2. Visualize yourself sitting comfortably, just as you are, and begin to open the crown chakra, seeing in your mind's eye a wonderful bright beam of light connecting you with the Source of all love and light. Imagine that your arms are reaching up into the light and see the energy flowing between yourself and the Divine. Bring the light down into your body, through your head, and consciously allow it to fill all your senses and your third eye, comfortably and safely.

3. Now breathe the light in through your ears and your nose, then breathe down through your throat, your neck, along your shoulders, your arms and out through your fingertips. As you breathe the light further down into your chest, see it filling your heart and your lungs. Watch the light flow down through your abdomen and pelvis, your spinal chord, hips and down through each leg to the tips of your toes.

4. Call upon Archangel Raphael and the Angels of Healing by saying, "Archangel Raphael, may I step into the presence of your Loving Light", and setting your intention on your Higher Self – lovingly and willingly accepting the Divine love and healing. Asking the angels to over-light your meditation, let them add their healing energy to your own.

5. Now take the light down into Mother Earth herself. Anchor the light through the soles of your feet, through the tips of your fingers and through your base chakra as you sit. Say three times: "Every cell of my body works in perfect harmony." Allow yourself to breathe for a moment with this feeling and imagine that, as you say this phrase, you can experience every cell tuning into the other, sending harmonious messages of love and acceptance throughout your body.

6. Now visualize a pale green light swirling as a mist around your feet and forming a beautiful ball of green light, like a wonderful orb of energy that stands at your feet, surrounding you with a sense of calm and balance, and watch as it starts to move slowly upwards around and through you.

7. Slowly, as you breathe the light upwards, sense the presence of one of the Angels of Healing offering you a gift. This is the first gift – a gift for your body. Accept it with gratitude, whatever it may feel like, whatever it may be. It could be a sensation, a word, an object or picture, a fragrance, shape or colour. Whatever it is, it is personally yours, for your body, your health. And it's from the Angels of Healing. Sense the gift – don't try to analyse or find meaning in it – but just hold on to it. Repeat again three times: "Every cell in my body works in perfect harmony."

8. Now watch as the ball of green healing energy rises up slowly with each breath over and through your body. Visualize it energizing and healing every organ, every bone, sinew and blood cell, every nerve and gland. Release any painful memories you are holding there into the green ball of light.

9. When the ball of light reaches your heart area, notice that it becomes a deeper emerald-green, and feel the intensity of the love you are being offered, allowing your heart to truly open, and ask that this Divine healing energy melt and clear away any pain or tension that you have been holding in this area of your body.

10. Trust that you are totally safe and deserve only pure loving, healing energy in your heart, letting go of any other feelings that no longer serve you. Repeat three times: "Every cell in my body works in perfect harmony."

11. As your heart opens and fills with emerald-green universal energy, you may sense the presence of another angelic being, even brighter than the last, with a spiritual gift, specifically for your heart. See, hear or feel the gift and accept it with love and gratitude to be observed more closely later. Sit with this feeling for a few moments and accept how truly loved and valued you really are.

12. Now watch as the green light ball continues to move slowly through and around your body as it passes further upwards around your arms and shoulders, neck and face until it reaches the crown at the top of your head. Inviting the light to heal and re-energize you, visualize the green light blending with a bright white light beam that connects you with the Divine Source. Repeat again three times, "Every cell in my body works in perfect harmony."

13. As you watch the lights blending and swirling together in a harmonious pattern, gaining brightness and loving energy, feel once again the presence of an angelic being of healing light offering you a third gift, for your soul. Sense the gift and sit for a moment of acceptance and loving gratitude, trusting that whatever you require for your healing and growth has been given to you, without conditions.

14. Thank the Divine and the angels from your heart, and as you watch it the green light is absorbed into the bright white light. See the beam as it narrows to a thread, connecting you always with the Source of all light and pure love.

15. Now breathe yourself back into your surroundings. Slowly grounding your energy back through your feet and hands, perhaps squeezing your fingers, or touching your face. And when you are ready, very slowly, open your eyes.

16. You might like to draw the symbols you have been given, or make a note of your gifts, and reflect on your emotions and feelings on completion of this meditation. Time taken now in processing your thoughts and recording them in your journal will be a valuable measure of your spiritual growth and development when you look back at a later date.

Working with the angels for holistic healing

Once you have become aware of the issues you need to work on, and have brought back some of the balance between body, mind, heart and soul through healing your body using the chakras, you can call on Raphael as a channel for Divine healing energy to help you heal others too.

You can do this on a personal or planetary level. Some of you probably already use daily prayer or send "distant" healing for the planet and for other people as well as healing for yourself. Some people have a natural ability and deep desire to work as healers. If you wish to be used as a channel for healing, you may have already become a Reiki healer, or are working with the Grace of the Holy Spirit as a spiritual healer. You may feel that you have a natural ability to heal people with your calm presence or some inner capacity and knowledge that you don't quite understand. I like to concentrate on calling in the Divine Light of the Holy Spirit, Jesus and Raphael and send out distant healing every Thursday. As this is Raphael's day it reminds me to keep the practice going.

It is believed by some that we are all capable of healing ourselves as well as others. Jesus the Essene and Master of Healing taught that whatever he could do, we could do also in His name, as long as we have a pure heart. As with all spiritual work, it is essential to study our intentions. With the best intentions in the world, we often have a hidden agenda, usually for what we believe to be the best for the one we are trying to heal – especially if it is someone close to us who is suffering. But we cannot impose our desired outcomes onto anyone else, and we must trust that whatever happens is part of their personal journey, and karma, and ask only for the best possible outcome for their highest good. In some cases we may take away their pain, ease their symptoms and make them much better – even cured. But if they haven't dealt with the underlying emotional issues, then unfortunately the health issue will most certainly return.

There are many things you can do to start working as a "healer". If you wish to invoke angelic healing energies by inviting Archangel Raphael to use you as a channel of healing energy, all you really need is a genuine desire to be of true service. You can do this in one of several ways.

1. Be of service to the community

You might like to offer yourself in service to the whole of humanity, or the planet itself. You can link with like-minded friends to send out prayers at a certain time of the day. This has enormously beneficial effects.

The news agency Reuters held an investigation in which it noted a substantial reduction in crime in Los Angeles following a sustained group prayer instigated by the mayor. The power of prayer has been seen to make a great difference to the peace and calm of many towns, and for this reason, as well as spiritual communion, many churches, groups and organizations have linked together in this way.

There are also many spiritually orientated groups that you may like to join on the internet. You have probably already seen that the author, songwriter and acclaimed "prayer-troubadour" James Twyman, for example, holds worldwide online prayer groups of thousands of people, which raise awareness for peace projects around the globe.

Another of these is an international organization called Triangles, part of the Arcane School with a charity called World Goodwill, which is based in London and New York. They invite people to get together in "threes" once a day to say a short prayer called the "Great Invocation". The triangle and number of people in each group holds the intention, the energy and the mystical power of three, which intensifies and magnifies the power of the words of the prayer.

2. Absent healing

You might like to call upon the angels to be present with you as you send absent healing to those you know who are sick or troubled. This works particularly well if you prearrange with the recipient when you will give and they will receive.

After completing a "Healing with Angels" course I once sent healing at a prearranged time every day to a friend in his sixties who had broken his arm. He had been told it might take several weeks to heal. But, after only three weeks of receiving the healing energy, the doctors were astounded at how quickly his arm was healing when he went for a check-up.

---

3. Hands-on healing

When you are present with a person whom you feel needs healing energy, you can ask if you can place your hands on their head or shoulders or wherever they are feeling pain. Then simply open your heart to receive the loving, healing energies of the angels, asking that they use you as a channel to pour out healing wherever it is most needed. Always thank the angels at the end of the session and, as I suggest below, you'll need to learn how to intentionally "close" and protect your own energies so that you are not left depleted.

GIVING HEALING

Even though many churches offer "hands-on" healing as part of their service from members of the congregation, and you can certainly give genuine and effective healing to your friends and loved ones, if you are going to do this regularly, or indeed for financial reward, then you'll need professional training. This would include important teaching in all aspects of healing work, such as the flow of energy between you and the sick person, self-protection and the current requirements of insurance, etc.

Natural deep healing

Perhaps not surprisingly, the element associated with Raphael is water – the source of all life and the element that holds our heartfelt emotions. Water feeds us, soothes us, heals us, bathes us, quenches our thirst, keeps our bodies in working order and without it we cannot survive. And whether it's a calm lake or the raw energy of the ocean, we tend to be drawn to it. I imagine that, like me, you let out a sigh of relief when walking on a beach or along a canal bank. I find it serves as a reminder of the healing that is intrinsic in all of nature.

If you spend time gazing in wonder at the bright stars or the enigmatic beauty of a new moon, you are engaging in a spiritual practice because you are tuning into the cosmos. If the amazing cloudscapes catch your eye with shapes that seem to bring messages from the angels, you are engaging in a spiritual practice.

These connections with the natural world balance our energy, bring us back to our centre and are deeply healing. There are no specifically religious connotations, yet it is in these moments that we can find a sacred connection with creation, which might be described as a deeply spiritual experience. Every cell in our body is created from the same chemical components as those that make up the Earth herself. So when we feel that connection, it is like our mother nourishing us. So remember to stop and give thanks to the angels and elements for the emotional energy flowing between the power of water and our soul!

PRACTICE 4
Water healing

There is something energizing about finding the source of a bubbling stream; something soothing about sitting by a flowing river; something exciting about witnessing the power of the crashing ocean waves. Sometimes we need to go outdoors and find some peace and here's a lovely exercise for working with water to cleanse, heal and soothe your body.

1. Sit comfortably, with your back straight and feet firmly on the floor. Breathe into your inner sacred space and imagine your feet sending roots down into the earth.

2. Relax as you breathe down into your hara and imagine yourself becoming transparent. You are a beautiful, crystal-clear version of yourself, a "you-shaped" vase.

3. As you breathe, visualize drawing cool, clear, pure water up through the roots in the soles of your feet. Feel it cleansing, purifying and healing as it fills your legs and slowly rises up your body. Allow the water to slowly fill your cells, replacing all negativity it may find there.

4. As the water flows through you it might slow down or change colour in some way. Try not to analyse why it is getting stuck, simply send your love to that part of your body.

5. Take your time. Once the water has reached your head it may metaphorically burst through your crown and create a beautiful, rainbow-coloured fountain showering sparkles of crystal-clear healing water all around you and through your aura.

6. When you are ready, take your focus back to your feet and ground yourself. Take a few deep breaths and open your eyes.

You might like to journal how this exercise makes you feel.

DAILY PRAYER

Dear Archangel Raphael and the Angels of Healing,

Thank you for your presence in my life.

Surround me in your glorious healing Light so that I may reflect your healing love to everyone I meet.

Please use me in service as a channel of Divine healing energy. That I may be an agent of healing in some way, either in my silent thoughts, words or deeds throughout each day, being open to every opportunity, with everyone I meet.

I ask you to guide my actions in relation to others, always seeking the positive in every situation, always intentionally focusing on the highest good of every outcome.

Heal, strengthen and consecrate my heart that my very nature may be loving, accepting and kind, united with all beings, visible and invisible in the realms of love and light, seeing joy in myself and others.

May my heart light brightly shine, so that I may give, and receive, from the depths of my being in truth, goodness and love.

Thank you.

Amen.

STEP 5

LEARN TO LOVE
EXPLORING THE GOLDEN THREAD WITH ARCHANGEL CHAMUEL

"When we are seeing through the eyes of love, there can be no judgement, no criticism and no condemnation, we are then living in the light."

Dr Wayne Dyer

ANGEL ASSOCIATIONS

Attributes: Love, Tolerance, Forgiveness, Kindness, Gratitude, Self-love
Colour: Keeper of the Pink Flame
Crystals: Rose Quartz, Pink Rhodochrosite
Day of the week: Tuesday
Planetary association: Venus
Element: Water
Ashram: Above St Louis, Missouri, USA

As we make our journey onwards, raising our vibration, lifting our spirits, we realize that the only true life-giving and sustaining emotion is love; this is the Golden Thread that connects us and the key to opening the next door.

So far Gabriel has nudged us awake and helped us step onto, or perhaps even stumble across, our true soul path. Jophiel has illuminated all those light-bulb moments, revealing them to be Divine inspiration, and has shown us with discernment, wisdom and grace that our soul has a plan – all we need to do is intuitively follow it. Archangel Michael has reminded us of how important psychic protection is and we have called upon his mighty sword to cut away anything that's been holding us back from living a purposeful life. And, finally, we've begun the healing process by connecting to Archangel Raphael's beneficent Light.

Step 5 is about deepening your understanding of true, universal, unconditional love and how to share loving-kindness throughout the world in harmony with the angels. Stepping into the beautiful rose-pink energy of Archangel Chamuel, the practical exercises in this chapter show you how to:

- Love and respect yourself, strengthen your self-esteem, gain confidence and honesty in relationships as well as help you to think, speak and act lovingly in all situations.
- Become conscious of what love means to you.
- Safely reflect on those aspects of yourself that you may find difficult to love, without judgement.
- Inject real love into your relationships, including close family and friendships, and help you to attract a loving relationship if you are seeking romance.
- Use forgiveness techniques to practise self-love and compassion.
- Send loving-kindness out into the larger community and the Universe.

Defining love

Talking of love and learning how to enhance feelings of loving energy does not mean being overly sentimental. Working with angels to develop your ability to love without question does not represent weakness. Nor does it mean you need to adopt any sickly sweetness. Being more tolerant and accepting of others, without trying to change them, means we are developing spiritually; we are becoming more aware and in control of our own reactions.

The angels are warriors of the Light; there is nothing weak or "soft" about them! Real love is strong and supportive, it is honest, authentic and means loving without the need to control others, allowing those we love to be free. Real love is nurturing without smothering; it is shining your Light and being true to your soul.

PRACTICE 1
Stepping into Chamuel's angelic love

This guided meditation will allow you to step into Chamuel's beautiful rose-coloured Light of love, which will help you create and heal all forms of love in your life.

If you need to refresh your memory about using the guided meditations, see Tools for Your Journey (page 17), or, if you prefer to listen to it as a meditation download, go to: www.AngelLight.co.uk/sevensteps.

1. Get comfortable and, if you choose, spend a few minutes breathing deeply before closing your eyes.
2. Starting with your feet, slowly scan your body so that with each exhalation you relax each set of muscles.

3. Begin by asking Archangel Chamuel and the Angels of Love to come closer to you, perhaps by saying, "Archangel Chamuel and the angels from the realm of pure Love, I ask that you come closer to me, that I might step into your Light. Thank you."

4. As you breathe slowly, deeply and gracefully, down into your lower abdomen, relax your body. Allow yourself to settle into a calm and meditative state.

5. Start the connection by imagining yourself surrounded by a beautiful pink light. Then, as you breathe, invite this pink light into your body, allowing it to fill your lungs and chest. Imagine your head, arms, body, lower abdomen, pelvic organs, legs and feet are filling with the beautiful, pure, pink, loving light with each breath.

6. Particularly notice if there are any areas of your body where the light does not seem to flow easily. Any dark or dense patches, or areas you find hard to visualize, and lovingly ask that these areas of your body receive the energy of the pink light of the angels. Concentrate your loving energy towards these areas of your body, thanking them for the hard work that they do and asking them to intuitively let you know what damage or painful memories they are holding. An answer may pop into your head: go with it and breathe the pink light deeply into that area. Allow the memory to be given to the Divine and the angels, releasing it and letting it dissolve in the light. (This may take practice if you are holding negative energy in parts of your body that give you pain or make you feel uncomfortable, perhaps because you do not like that part of your body.)

7. Smile inwardly, being gentle with yourself. Literally "lighten up" and allow yourself to let the pink light in. Imagine

that the pink light is also coming through your skin and you have a wonderful pink glow that is simultaneously surrounding you and coming through you. Imagine that your bloodstream, your muscles and sinews, your bones, brain – every tissue and every cell – is now being bathed in the loving pink light of the angels.

8. Now ask out loud that Archangel Chamuel and the Angels of Love help you to dissolve any feelings of low self-esteem, self-condemnation, selfishness and self-dislike. (Speaking it out loud has more effect because you are hearing your words yourself as well as sensing the thoughts in your head and it acts as a positive affirmation to your body.)

9. Ask them to help you reframe your self-belief patterns as you develop ways to create feelings of compassion, forgiveness, mercy, tolerance and gratitude instead. This is aimed towards your personal self, your physical body, your mind, spirit and soul.

10. Visualize the pink glow embracing you, filling you up and surrounding you, reaching out to either side of you. Once you feel it for yourself, you can choose to allow the same feelings to flow through you and then outwards to everyone that you meet.

11. If there is any part of you that still feels unsure or incapable of loving your true beautiful soul-self – or if you are still holding on to harmful addictive behaviours or aspects of your personality that create barriers between you and your loved ones – allow yourself to recognize it and own it. Just as we all like to celebrate our best, we each have a dark side too. The shadows of traits we would rather hide away, all our other shady bits of the past and rougher characteristics within our personality are ours as well. We must embrace the

shadows as well as the Light within our self because it is who we are ("warts and all", as the saying goes). Then, by taking full responsibility without blame or harsh self-judgement, we can make a choice to change. Don't fight any feelings that come bubbling up. Spiritual growth can be tough medicine sometimes. Even those who have been putting spirituality into their lives for decades still need help with it from time to time.

12. You might like to say a prayer to the Angels of Love under the guidance of Archangel Chamuel to bring about the changes you need – something like: "Archangel Chamuel and the Angels of Love, I send my prayer from my heart, in pure love. I ask that all negative thoughts or behaviours that are self-negating or unloving be released now. Please fill me with your love that I may reflect your Light to everyone around me, with no conditions. May your blessing of love flow freely now. Thank you."

13. Now repeat the following fiat three times: "In the name of the Divine, I AM that I AM, in the name of Archangel Chamuel and the Angels of Love... Be gone forces of Anti-Love!" (You can also use this whenever you feel a dip in self-esteem.)

14. Set your intention to receive. As you ask with true honesty and with an open heart, believe and trust that it is already happening now. At the same time, ask Chamuel to help you to attract loving, mutually beneficial and supportive relationships into your life for the greatest good of the highest purpose. Affirmations are great for supporting this kind of request because as you use the affirmation more regularly you hear it yourself and, as we already know, energy follows thought. Your powerful thoughts tap into the universal mind and, hey presto,

just like magic, it starts to happen – as long as the energy is pure and you are willing to believe. Use whichever affirmation speaks you more strongly: "*I am ready to love myself and others fully with a pure heart*" or "*I am open to attract mutually loving and beneficial relationships into my life now.*"

15. Sit with that thought for as long as you are able to. Envisage loving energy passing between you and all your friends and family members. Envisage all discussions having a friendly and mutually beneficial outcome. Envisage people smiling at you and welcoming you wherever you go. See yourself free from any addictive patterns, and see the glow from your heart becoming stronger and stronger.

16. This light in your heart is with you always. Whenever your self-esteem is low, or you are tempted to be too harsh on yourself or others, reconnect to this beautiful pink light in your heart and fill your energy with it, calling again on the assistance of the angels of Chamuel.

17. Breathing slowly, deeply, deliberately, allow yourself to be back in the present moment. Bring yourself into your own space, your own room, breathing normally. Feel your body: solid, present and fully grounded. Very slowly, when you're ready, open your eyes.

I remember an elderly aunt once telling me that you shouldn't use the word "love" unless you mean it. Her staunch Methodist and Victorian values clearly restricted her verbal expression of love, even though she was one of the kindest women I ever knew. Has the "L" word become overused and misunderstood? I prefer to think that it is a really good idea to put the energy of the word out into the ether as often as possible. After all, we know that energy follows thought, so perhaps the more we say it the more loving we may actually become. The more Light we shine, the brighter it gets!

Wherever we look – in books and movies, on TV and social media feeds, throughout religious and spiritual writings – we're told that love is all there is. And it is the most important part of life. We are asked to love one another, to love ourselves and to be unconditional about it – but it's so hard to get right, isn't it?

A child will learn love by feeling it first from their mother, then by watching the relationship between their parents, siblings and family. A young adult modifies and develops that deep-rooted learning by experimenting quite naturally throughout the teenage years in friendships and youthful romances. We all feel a need to be loved. Yet, if we have been betrayed, abandoned or abused then love can be a negative experience and we might learn ways of manipulating this natural and human need. But even neediness, self-centredness, attention-seeking, control, loneliness and dependency are all still expressions of love. It's also true that the most vulnerable and in need of love are also at the highest risk of being exploited. There are so many aspects and definitions of love that it can sometimes make us wonder whether we're talking about the same emotion. Let's take a closer look.

What does love *really* mean to you? Are you *in love* with someone special right now? If so would that be *true* love, *possessive* love, *lustful* love, *erotic* love or *real* love? Or are you waiting and hoping for that person to come into your life? If you have just come through a bereavement or divorce, you may be thinking you might never find true love again. In which case, the loss of love you are grieving may fill you with a need for *supportive, nurturing* love.

Do you have family you adore, friends and colleagues you would do anything for? So what kind of love is this? Is this a kind of protective, loyal, brother/sisterly, mother/fatherly kind of family love?

Do you actually *feel* loved, cherished and valued? But then, I wonder, does this sense of self-love need acceptance, acknowledgement, approval, admiration and gratitude from other people?

Maybe you can answer yes to some of the above questions. Perhaps none of them resonate. In any case, you may be wondering, is love really so important?

Well, actually, yes it is. Science has proven that we need love to survive as healthy human beings. Brain scans show that the brain volume of a child can be shaped by experience and a child that has been severely neglected, physically as well as emotionally, can have a dramatically reduced brain size. Children's brains actually grow when they are cuddled, loved and nurtured. What's more, the studies into epigenetics have shown that how much nurture we receive as children can not only affect us but also be passed down via our genes to our offspring and their offspring.[1]

And, if we need any more reason to turn towards love, then recent research at Harvard University indicates that adults in loving relationships are healthier, while adopting a more loving and compassionate lifestyle can have beneficial effects on long-term health.[2-4] In other words, we remain well when we are in a loving, mutually supportive relationship with another. (Even if that "other" is a pet.)

Any way that you can put "Love into Action" means you are creating a more heavenly world.

Whether we accept or reject love depends on the nurture we received as a child and our subsequent experiences of love. But when our aim is to love unconditionally then it means upping our game – not just giving and receiving love – but engaging with a multidimensional emotion, including even those whom we intensely dislike or who are unkind, or even abusive.

PRACTICE 2
Defining Love

Consider the following questions about love and reflect on how you feel and how your body responds to each. This isn't a quiz; there are no points for right or wrong answers. And it's not an exercise in self-judgement, simply a method of self-reflection to help you become conscious of what love is to you.

Bring something or someone to mind as an example of how you would respond in any of the following situations, and answer the following questions by looking deeply into your heart and answering honestly:

1. How easy is it for you to actually love someone when you dislike their way of life?
2. How hard is it for you to love someone when their behaviour embarrasses or humiliates you?
3. Are you able to express criticism in a loving way?
4. When you are angry do you ever resort to attacking the personality of your offender, maybe through name-calling, rather than dealing with the situation?
5. Would you say truthfully that you are able to remain dignified when someone you love disappoints you? Or do you add drama, shout, cry or make demands?

6. If "being loved is being loving", how easy is it to love those people around you who press your buttons?

Learning to love unconditionally

It might seem that unconditional love is too difficult. But, learning to love with Chamuel as your guide – no matter how you might have been hurt in the past – it is possible to heal your heart and love openly and unconditionally. So let's start by exploring the different dimensions of love.

PRACTICE 3
Meditating on the "Dimensions of Love"

The following practice can help you to connect and explore your feelings about love, whether it's something that comes naturally to you or feels as though it's an enigma.

If you need to refresh your memory about using the guided meditations, see Tools for Your Journey (page 17).

1. Get comfortable and, if you choose, spend a few minutes breathing deeply in the light of your candle before closing your eyes.
2. When you are fully relaxed, imagine walking into a building, such as an office block. Start by finding a staircase, or stepping into an elevator, and go up to the fourth floor. Here you arrive at a long corridor of identical doors. Each of the doors has a different sign on it, and you notice that they represent different emotions: jealousy, fear, envy, humour, sadness and joy. Walk along the

corridor and, observing the door names as you pass, stop at the door that displays the sign "LOVE".

3. Spend some time vividly imagining the door – its handle, its colour and its inscription. Behind this door there are many different representations of love – a whole universe of love – including all sorts of people, beings, objects, memories, situations, states of emotion and consciousness.

4. Now open the door and let the first spontaneous impressions come up without deciding beforehand what they should be. They may appear in any form, perhaps as an image, a word, a physical sensation, a sound, a smell... and so on.

5. Gradually get accustomed to the universe behind that door. Explore it. Whatever you find, whether pleasant or unpleasant, try these two objectives. First, look clearly and without judgement at whatever you see; don't rush away, but take some time with any image that appears. Give the image the opportunity to reveal itself fully to you. Second, realize that each image (whatever it may be) is only one among the vast number of unquantifiable images and manifestations that can be connected with love. Tell yourself: "This is also an aspect of the vast universal love," then move on to the next image, or thought, until you are ready to leave.

6. Come away and close the door. Return to the lift or stairs and come back down to the ground floor. Bring the images to mind that you have found and write them down. You might want to work out the significance, the meaning (which may be symbolic) and connection to your life. It might be helpful to draw what you have visualized if you are feeling creative.

7. Say the following affirmation, out loud if possible: "*I increase my understanding of all aspects of love whenever I connect to Divine loving Light. I am ready and willing to accept all aspects of love, without judgement.*"

8. Breathing slowly, deeply, deliberately, allow yourself to be back in the present moment. Bring yourself into your own space, your own room, breathing normally. Feel your body: solid, present and fully grounded. Very slowly, when you're ready, open your eyes.

Loving-kindness

If we accept that perhaps, under some circumstances, we are not always the most loving person, it follows that we can become more lovable when we are loving towards ourselves. This doesn't mean you have to suppress anger or disappointment, and it absolutely doesn't imply that you should accept bad behaviour or abuse or stay in toxic situations that harm your wellbeing. It simply means that there may be a different, more loving way to deal with the situation, or with other people; a way that reflects our Light in a more positive way, without being subjected to any form of toxicity or abuse. In that scenario, stepping away is often the kindest action for all concerned.

If being kind is being loving then surely kindness is the same vibration as love. Performing or being on the receiving end of simple acts of kindness always makes you feel good. It raises your self-esteem and gives you an inner glow that opens the heart and increases your aura – filling it with high vibrational energy. These don't have to be grand gestures of largesse, just whatever resonates with you. So, for example, you might choose to buy a hot drink for a homeless person, bake a cake for a neighbour or join a community project to plant seeds or trees – the options are endless. And if you've always been told that giving is it's own reward but never fully believed it, studies have shown that kindness not only begets more kindness, but also reduces stress, increases wellbeing and even longevity.[5]

Use the following affirmations to remind you of the power of giving more love and kindness:

As I open my heart with kindness and love, the more kindness and love is returned to me.

When I share my loving energy with others, kindness and love flows in abundance in return.

Love is the highest vibrational emotion you can feel. When you are inspired to follow an inner spiritual calling, whether from the angelic realms or your Higher Self, you are definitely being called to serve the highest good. As you raise your own vibration, your energy reflects out into the world and your smallest acts, even a simple smile, bring love into other people's lives. Jesus, Buddha and all the other great spiritual teachers emphasized the need for love, and they knew that this vibration was universal – a cosmic energy of creation.

However, as I mentioned earlier in the chapter, low self-esteem can prevent you from receiving and giving unconditional love, and this is where you often need to develop strategies for self-love.

Self-love

Not everyone has low self-esteem, but self-love is not very common, especially among very sensitive souls who have perhaps given much of their power away to more dominant people in their life, and then felt bad about not being able to stand up for themselves. Stress and challenging life events, such as illness and loss, can also damage self-esteem. Signs of low self-esteem are wide-ranging and can lead to depression and anxiety, as well as unhelpful addictions. In my work, I am always saddened that it is so often a lack of self-esteem and self-love that has such a deep effect on how we heal and how we conduct our relationships.

> You are a beautiful, unique human being, loved for your self,
> created and fashioned with LOVE by the One creator... You
> are a part of the Divine plan... Why would you not be loved?

The following three practices, when used regularly, can really help you step into another bright light, one that radiates from self-love.

Loving thoughts

Regularly using affirmations of self-worth can help shift our energy from feeling bad about ourselves to an attitude of self-care. So affirmations such as: *"I love and respect myself"* or *"I am lovable and lovely, and only attract loving people into my life"* may seem strange at first, but the more you hear those words the more you begin to engage with them. The affirmation resonates at a cellular level and you start to believe it.

The energy of Chamuel is nothing less than sublime and connecting with Chamuel's Light in Practice 1 (see page 135) will help you direct loving thoughts towards yourself.

> ## INNER SIGHT
>
> The more you work with the angel energies the easier it will become to visualize with your inner sight and intuitively "feel" their energetic colours surrounding you.

As the energy of those loving thoughts spreads through your environment, it creates a happier life, which in turn increases your wellbeing and self-esteem, and so you love more. You know how it feels to spend time in the home of a happy family and to take something lovely away when your leave? Imagine the effect this feeling would have if it were inside you. You would be able to send it out in waves to everyone around the world.

Now imagine what it would be like if every human being expressed themselves in positive language and with kindness, so that we felt at home wherever we were. Imagine if the Golden Thread of Love was woven throughout education so there was no bullying and all children were taught in an environment of love rather than targets of achievement. If everyone in the healthcare profession was valued, so that patients were treated holistically. If politicians and governments always negotiated for the highest possible outcome of everyone globally.

It all starts here: with self-love and by taking small steps until you can run. Use the following affirmations to help support you:

As I generously spread my Light with love I am co-creating a peaceful world.

I am able to see only the best in everyone I meet, creating harmony in every situation.

*I am love and Light and I send it forwards
into my day, surrounding everyone I meet
with blessings.*

Forgiveness

I shared a forgiveness exercise in Step 4 (see Practice 1, page 135) and we'll delve deeper still into forgiveness in Step 6 (when we'll work with the transformational energies of Zadkiel) because forgiveness is an ongoing process on our journey into Light and vital in self-love.

Learning to work alongside loving angels and develop a deeper connection with their energy by using the meditations, prayers, visualizations, crystals and so on all adds to the continuous weaving of the Golden Thread of Divine Love within our world.

Our thoughts and actions don't just affect us but also all other sentient beings, nature and every part of life. Whether we are awake to this or not, it is happening in every moment in the way we project our thoughts as words and deeds. Just as a simple example, think of a smile. When we smile at a stranger (and whether or not they smile back), it has a positive effect. They may well go on to recognize the friendly gesture and pass it on to another person they meet. Why? Simply because that smile has the power to change energy.

We co-create our entire reality because ultimately we are all part of one world, one great cosmic Universe. It is a given that as we grow up we learn to take responsibility for our own decisions in life, but within the realms of spiritual development we next learn to take the bigger step of accepting that this is not just personal, but universal. Once we acknowledge this, we are able to take more responsibility for the part we play, in our immediate relationships, at work, in the home and out into the greater environment: our world.

This acceptance of the role we play in every life is expressed in a beautiful spiritual practice from Hawaii. Known as *Ho'oponopono* (ho-o-pono-pono), it is a practice of reconciliation and forgiveness from the ancient belief system called Huna. *Ho'oponopono* means "to make right", specifically with the ancestors and all people with whom you have relationships.

More recently the practice has been brought to light by the US author Joe Vitale (who took part in the film called *The Secret)*. Vitale heard of a psychotherapist, Dr Len in Hawaii, who cured a group of criminals in a psychiatric prison. He found the story incredible and at first wondered if it was just an urban myth. After deeper investigation, however, he found the story to be true. He was amazed at the results and started to put the same principles into practice – with phenomenal results. Vitale made a practice of saying, "I'm sorry, I love you" to himself in situations when someone had done something to upset or annoy him, rather than react or confront the other person. Soon he found situations reversing, and disagreeable relationship issues reconciled. Dr Len's explanation is that there is no "out there", only an "inside you", and that to heal the world you have to start by loving it, and that truly begins... surprise, surprise... by learning to love yourself.

PRACTICE 4
Practising *Ho'oponopono*

Try this simple yet incredibly powerful forgiveness practice for yourself.

1. Get comfortable and take a few moments to focus on your breath before calling in the Archangel Chamuel to surround you in angelic pink loving energy to strengthen your own.
2. Light a candle, perhaps hold a piece of rose quartz crystal, and say these phrases with a particular issue in mind: "I am sorry. Forgive me. I love you. Thank you."
3. Keep a journal of the outcome. You'll be astonished at the effect after practice.

I have used *Ho'oponopono* with challenging people and situations I have found extremely hurtful. Taking these active steps and developing spiritual practices that include gratitude and forgiveness always makes a difference. It enables us to embody the spirit of our beautiful soul. It gives us the power to take action, as Ghandi encouraged in his famous words: "Be the change you want to see in the world."

Stop comparing yourself and recognize your achievements

Most of us at some point will stop and wonder what we have done with our lives. It might make us feel small, not good enough, not *spiritual* enough, or wish to be like someone else. We may feel as if, while others have seemingly done great things or gained success in their life, we have been wasting our time.

But if you analyse your timeline from Step 1 (see Practice 4, page 48), you will see that you have plenty of achievements to be proud of. This is not just an exercise in polishing the ego, but an honest self-valuation. It is important for you to know and accept that every single one of us has, in some way, made a difference to another person's life.

Have you created something beautiful? Do you have friends? Do you have a home you share with others? Have you learned to swim, ride a bicycle, drive or cook? Have you climbed a mountain, passed an exam, earned a degree, learned to speak another language, given birth? Any of these are achievements and I am certain that, once you start to think about it, you'll be able to create a whole list of your own.

When I look back to my early nursing career in the 1970s, we still rolled washed crêpe bandages for re-use. It was a seemingly insignificant task, often given to the junior on the ward, but if it wasn't done, the senior trained nurses wouldn't be able to change the dressings following surgery. Remember: every act carries its own significance; every little job done with love makes a difference to someone, even if it may seem trivial to you.

PRACTICE 5
Developing unconditional self-love

Here is another guided meditation exercise to help raise your self-esteem. It is so important that you feel good about yourself without constantly seeking approval from others. The angels love you unconditionally: can you honestly say that you feel that way about yourself?

If you need to refresh your memory about using the guided meditations, see Tools for Your Journey (page 17).

1. Get comfortable and begin by breathing slowly and deeply. Breathe down into your lower abdomen and hold your breath for a couple of seconds, then release the breath and let go of all the tension in your body.

2. Imagine a bright light swirling into the room like a mist, and choose a favourite colour as the light gets brighter, surrounding you with its beautiful energy.

3. Breathe the light into your body with each breath. Imagine it filling every cell until it begins to seep through the pores of your skin. Feel the light shining within you and around you.

4. Notice the colour of the light change to a soft pink colour as it starts to move in a circular swirling movement around your legs. Say to yourself three times: "I am safe, and I trust my connection with the Divine Light."

5. As the light swirls around your lower abdomen, feel and engage with the energy of this beautiful positive light and say to yourself three times: "I let go of all past negative experiences that no longer serve me. I release all negative thoughts about my self into the light."

6. As the light swirls upwards around your middle (solar plexus), say to yourself: "I have clear boundaries, I respect my freedom to be, feel and express my own truth."

7. Imagine the light now flowing around your heart. At this point your guardian angel comes closer to you and as he/she blesses you, open your heart, allowing the love to flow between you and your angel. Say to yourself three times: "I am loved unconditionally, I do not have to do or be anything other than I am now to be loved."

8. The light now moves upwards and swirls around your neck and head, clearing all negative thoughts and leaving only positive energy with you as it permeates through you.

SEVEN STEPS INTO ANGEL LIGHT

9. Thank the angel, and your self, for taking part as you visualize the light fading and now leaving the room.
10. Breathe slowly and, as you release the out breath, bring your energy back into your personal space, knowing you are truly loved and cherished.

Love in every part of life

A loving relationship with someone special, who returns our love, is fulfilling and nourishing, but shouldn't all our relationships be like that? Putting love, consideration and acceptance without judgement into all our dealings with others brings a more comfortable and harmonious relationship with everyone.

So many people have written to me over the years about their troubles in love. If I do card readings at festivals, people come along wanting to be told they will find their perfect love soon. Yet all the spiritual teachers advise us that in order to find real love we must first learn to know and love our self.

There are three names for love: "philia" is the love we feel for our friends and family, "eros" is the love we feel for our partners, while "agape" is the kind of love we call unconditional, or universal. This is the love we feel for the Divine.

As well as learning to love and accept who we are, we must also discover forgiveness (as I described earlier) to find out what love really is. Learning to love unconditionally, and to accept other people in our life without trying to change them, is one of life's greatest lessons. The other is learning to love and accept ourselves and bringing self-love into our daily practice.

I remember one of my students, a junior schoolteacher from Australia, remarking that she found it heart-breaking that so many children at the London school where she was teaching described themselves – at the age of eight – as "stupid". They had no self-belief. When she introduced topics that were a little stretching, the first reaction of a high proportion of children in the class was, "Miss, I can't do that." So she began to introduce mirrors into the classroom. Every time a child in her class achieved something, whether it was in a lesson or an interaction with another child, she would instruct them to hold a mirror up to their face and to say to their own reflection: "I'm really proud of you, you did really well today."

Life can take its toll. We know that how kind or difficult our life has been to us shows in our demeanour, posture and the lines on our face. We have also learned from Step 4 that healing is reflected in the state of our body, mind and spirit. What we need to do now, having decided to change our self-depreciating behaviour patterns, is to learn to love and appreciate ourselves just as we are now – without blame or harsh self-judgement. After all, we are still just as beautiful, fabulous, gifted and loved in the eyes of the Divine and the angels. Whatever we feel we have done, however we may have met life's challenges, our soul light is still seen by the angels as a pure, shining light.

Depression and low self-esteem dim our Light. When we are sick or in danger, this same inner light sends out sparks like lightning forks. It's this disjointed and disharmonious energy that is picked up by the angels, whose powerful loving, healing and protective energy rushes in to help by surrounding our own, to give support. They do this because of love. Love is the vibration of the angelic realms, and whether we truly understand it or not, there is no price attached to it – no hidden agenda.

I once heard an American speaker demonstrate this by taking a $50 bill out of his pocket. "Who would like this beautiful crisp new $50?" he asked the audience. Silence prevailed as clearly everyone thought it was a trick question. Then several hands shot into the air. He then squashed and screwed up the note between his hands. Straightening it out, he asked the same question again. There was a pause, but slowly hands were raised, one by one. They could clearly see it was the same $50, just now a bit crumpled. Then the speaker dropped the note onto the floor and trod on it as if putting out a cigarette butt. Then, picking it up and lifting it in the air, he asked: "Now who wants it?" Cautiously one or two hands were raised. The same happened after he had rolled the note between his fingers, tearing it slightly across the corner.

"Do you get my point?" the speaker asked. "The note was pristine, shiny and new not long ago. It has become creased and wrinkled, downtrodden, crushed and torn... spoiled perhaps by carelessness and rough treatment. Yet it is still the same $50, with the same value as it had in the beginning."

Life might seem to treat us roughly sometimes. We become worn and creased by time, and some of us may indeed be downtrodden, abused and feel as if we have lost part of who we were originally. But are we not the same loveable, valuable, bright and shiny soul that we were at birth? Often we give away our power and allow circumstances or other people to diminish our sense of self-worth, to lower our self-esteem. We may have learned not to accept our loveliness; perhaps we feel worthless. It is time to completely reverse that now. We ARE loveable. We have great value (all of us) and we are definitely loved!

PRACTICE 6
Discovering the real you

It's easy to slip into the same old negative language to talk to yourself, and this simple but fun exercise serves as a good reminder of all your wonderful attributes.

Write out each letter of the alphabet and think of an adjective for every letter to describe the real *you*. Remember: only positive words and no false humility. Here are a few suggestions to start you off:

- Accepting, attractive, awake...
- Benevolent, beautiful, brave...
- Courageous, caring, calm...
- Devoted, daring, dynamic...
- Energetic, enthusiastic, engaging...
- Faithful, generous, honest...
- Intelligent, joyful... kind... likeable, and so on and so on.

Some letters are more difficult than others – I tried this and have to admit I got stuck a couple of times! – but stretching my vocabulary was a great achievement in itself.

What would love say?

Let me remind you of the quote at the beginning of the chapter: "When we see through the eyes of love, there can be no judgement, no criticism and no condemnation, we are then living in the light." And as a last thought on this particular step, I'd like to add something my father once said when I was in a very difficult and challenging situation: "If 'Love' was here, a living person talking to you about this difficult issue… what do you think Love would say?"

DAILY PRAYER

Dear Archangel Chamuel,

May the universal and boundless grace of the Divine's love reflect off the angels and surround me.

May your affection enfold, support, nurture and inspire me.

May your strength be my strength.

May your Divine Light be my Divine Light.

May I serve as you serve.

May your Grace be my grace.

May your Love ever be my love.

Thank you.

Amen

STEP 6

TRANSFORMATION
YOUR PERSONAL METAMORPHOSIS
WITH ARCHANGEL ZADKIEL

"What the caterpillar calls the end of the world the master calls a butterfly."

Richard Bach

Each step we have taken so far has strengthened commitment, challenged ideas and deepened the connection to our personal spiritual impulse. We have picked up the Golden Thread interwoven through each step and gathered Divine Light along our journey. Now we are fully awake to the call of our soul's potential and ready to accept the angelic energies guiding us.

As I described earlier in the book, the light we see around us is a reflection of all the shades of the colour spectrum (see Introduction, page 10). The human eye picks out seven clear colours of the magnificent rainbow, for example when the sun shines through a droplet of water or a crystal, even though there are thousands of different shades within each arc.

Throughout the Seven Steps, we have been opening our hearts and minds to the Archangels and the particular qualities of their "flames of light". We have been bringing these spiritual qualities together and blending them with our own energy. Now, if you are willing to use them – by adding your unique gifts with integrity – then now is the time to begin actively and consciously joining in. By building up your confidence through spiritual practice, you can share this light throughout the world in your daily life. The practical exercises in this step will help you to:

- Cleanse and purify your energetic connection and so raise your energy vibration.
- Create a "happy anchor" to transform negativity into joy whenever you feel the need.
- Let go of judgement and fear, embrace joy and a sense of liberation.
- Establish a mindfulness practice to increase your awareness and consciousness.
- Use the violet flame for forgiveness.
- Begin a loving-kindness practice.

Discovering the transformational Light of Zadkiel

Archangel Zadkiel brings all the positive power of the Violet Flame into our lives (see Tools for Your Journey, page 16). This powerful light source can transform or *transmute* energy from negative to positive. Zadkiel has the role of Keeper of the Violet Flame, the energy of which we can call upon to help us fully dissolve painful memories and support us in changing negative thoughts, behaviour patterns and fears into positive life-force energy.

If we acknowledge that most of us have personalities tinged with some form of negativity towards some individuals – such as thoughts or actions related to greed, jealousy or judgement – we can also make the choice to let these feelings be transmuted. In terms of our karmic experience, this means that others are less likely to judge us and we'll enjoy more positive experiences. (Remember, what goes around comes around!)

As you begin to work with the powerful influence of Zadkiel, you may also see a clearer reason for being where you are: more clues to your soul purpose, even if you can't work out what that is right now. Your lifestyle, including your job or career – indeed, *everything* you have created for yourself – reflects the calling of your soul, and the Ray or Flame associated with your personal soul vibration. If you doubt that, then look at it this way: if you have always had a strong drive to pursue a certain career and are happy and fulfilled, then clearly it is right for you. However, even if you feel you are in a situation you dislike at the moment, perhaps because there are people there who annoy you, there will most certainly be lessons or challenges you have drawn into your life for a real reason.

For example, if you are resonating with the violet colour and the attributes of the transformational energy of Zadkiel, whether or not you are working in your ideal profession, you will have an interest in issues of freedom (whether personal or global) and aspects of culture, refinement and diplomacy. Your current situation may be teaching you tolerance, forgiveness and serving others within some kind of discipline. Maybe the lesson is in having the confidence to follow your inner calling (that spiritual impulse again) and be "liberated" from something that doesn't suit you. Have you thought that perhaps your Light is needed in that place? Perhaps you are an agent of change. For that is exactly the energy of this particular powerful angelic being.

Once you feel ready to raise your vibration closer to the bright true spiritual being you were born to be, you will definitely feel drawn towards Zadkiel's vibration at some point. He will enfold you in the transformational energy of the Violet Flame and transmute all your thoughts and actions into joy. When this happens, your perception of the way things are begins to change (slowly at first), and although you may well have your faults, you are able to notice them as an "observer" rather than as a strict parent or over-critical teacher. By building on the work you've done so far in self-love and appreciation, by letting go of any harsh self-judgements and taking a gentler and more loving attitude towards yourself, you will be able – if you choose – to make the change and fly, initiating your own personal metamorphosis.

Light is the Divine intelligence in all things.

PRACTICE 1
Letting go of judgement with Zadkiel's Violet Flame

This guided meditation will introduce you to Zadkiel's Violet Flame. It contains a rich and powerful process to help you let go of judgement and fear and fill you with joy and liberation. This practice can be cathartic for some; you may feel strong emotions as you release any negative feelings that you might have been holding on to for a very long time. You might even become quite euphoric or find yourself releasing tears of joy. Don't worry either way, both reactions are quite normal.

If you need to refresh your memory about using the guided meditations, see Tools for Your Journey (page 17), or, if you prefer to listen to it as a download, go to: www.AngelLight. co.uk/sevensteps.

1. Get comfortable and, if you choose, spend a few minutes breathing deeply before closing your eyes.
2. When you are ready, breathe into a slow and steady rhythm, relaxing and allowing the tension to leave you with every out breath. Feel each breath as it flows through your nostrils, down behind your throat, into your lungs, filling your chest and down into your lower abdomen. Allow yourself to sink into the chair, or the floor – wherever you are sitting. Breathing in and out, slowly and deeply, take each breath mindfully down into the core of your being.
3. Now say, either out loud or in your head, "Zadkiel, Zadkiel, Zadkiel, may I step into your Light" as you visualize the most beautiful, vivid violet light. See it surrounding you, growing richer and deeper in colour and intensity, perhaps mingling with other shades of purple and pink.
4. See the light swirling around you and imagine it as a blazing brilliance that penetrates through you. Within that intense light you begin to sense the presence of the great Archangel Zadkiel.
5. Now imagine that you're in the middle of a beautiful, rich violet flame of energy that rises all around you. Fill your heart with gratitude and know that you can safely let go

of all negativity into that purifying and transformational energy of Zadkiel and the angels of the Violet Flame.

6. Bring to mind any situation or personal behaviour patterns that you would like to change (as an observer, without judgement), and ask now that the angels transmute this negative thought into positive energy.

7. Affirm to yourself the desire to let go of these negative feelings, understanding that they affect your vibration and therefore hold back your spiritual development. Say, "Archangel Zadkiel, I let go of all negative emotions and I ask you to support me as you transmute them in this Violet Flame."

8. Bring to mind anything that you would like to see burnt away, dissolved in the powerful purifying light. It might be jealousy, impatience, greed, resentment, anger, judgement or bitterness. It may be a memory that causes a negative reaction in you, such as fear or sadness. Say to yourself, "I let go of all feelings I have of [name it]," and ask that it be purified and transformed now.

9. As you breathe rhythmically, say to yourself three times (or in sets of three, as many times as you wish): "I let go." Visualize all the negativity being dissolved by the violet light and imagine that it is being replaced by positive energy and many loving blessings.

10. Accept that this is done and say thank you to Zadkiel and his angels, affirming to yourself: "I AM freedom. I AM joy. I recognize my true value. I welcome joy. I welcome happiness and freedom. I AM freedom. I AM joy."

11. Feel the joy and the happiness of freedom that comes with positive loving energy and see it again swirling all around you in the shades of purple.

12. As you continue to breathe slowly and rhythmically, watch the violet light as it fades away. See it as a beautiful penetrating light moving from your crown, down your body, slowly subsiding until it seems to sink back into the Earth. Know that it has changed you. Know that negative thoughts have been purified and dissolved – transmuted by the powerful energy of the Violet Flame.

13. Breathing slowly, deeply, deliberately, allow yourself to be back in the present moment. Bring yourself into your own space, your own room, and breathe normally. Feel your body: solid, present and fully grounded. Very slowly, when you're ready, open your eyes.

This is a very powerful process. Once completed, please make sure you feel fully grounded (by swinging your arms around, jiggling your body or stomping your feet to get the circulation flowing) and drink a glass of water.

Tuning into the vibrational qualities of the Violet Flame, you may have found – either now or before reading this book – that you are particularly drawn to one of the specific "flame" colours and vibrational qualities. Violet, though sometimes described as purple, is very often the first colour people start to see when they learn to meditate. In spiritual terms it is associated with the angelic realms, and as well as having healing properties it is known as a regal colour. It can also be found in some of the most readily available natural sources.

Gems

It is no coincidence that amethyst is one of the most popular crystals. These gemstones have been highly valued since

Ancient Egyptian times, when they were engraved and worn as jewellery. The Ancient Greeks believed that amethysts had anti-intoxicating properties, while medieval European soldiers wore amethyst amulets for protection in battle. Beads of amethyst have been found in Anglo-Saxon graves in England, too. The reason for this popularity being that amethysts, then as now, were believed to heal people and keep them cool-headed. I for one recommend using this crystal in as many forms as you wish.

Bracelets made from pieces of amethyst are particularly powerful because they sit on a pulse point at your wrist, which takes their healing energy throughout your body. In the same way, an amethyst necklace can add healing energy to your heart chakra, and amethyst earrings to your third eye and crown.

When you first take a large piece of amethyst in your hands and observe it closely, you will see that it looks like a piece of ordinary rock on the underside: greyish with an uneven, rough surface. Turn it over, however, and on the inside you'll find it is filled with the most beautiful six-sided crystal clusters of varying shades of purple. I often use a piece at my workshops to demonstrate how we can hide our Light and our inner beauty inside what appears to be a very ordinary surface or exterior.

SELECTING AMETHYST CRYSTALS

When you buy a piece of amethyst, hold it in your hands and mentally tune into it; as a living energy form it will connect with your vibration and you can ask it to work with you.

Plants

Lavender oil, with its very distinctive scent, taken from a flowering plant with the same purple colour, has similar properties to amethyst, as it is also cooling and cleansing. As one of the only oils that can be put on the skin without first diluting with a carrier oil, it can be used in numerous ways, including as a natural first aid for stress, headaches, inflammation, bumps and bruises.

The sun's rays

The sun is essential to life on Earth. These ultraviolet rays were in very recent years believed to be harmful, but regular exposure to sunshine has now been found to be essential for our wellbeing. Not only for the production of vitamin D, which protects against bone diseases, but also because ultraviolet light raises serotonin levels in the brain[1] – the chemical that balances our mood and makes us feel happy.

Raising your vibration

As the Bearer of the Violet Flame, associated with a high spiritual vibrational frequency, working with Zadkiel is very attractive to those souls who desire self-realization in this lifetime. Just like the ancient mystics, some of us can practise "Divine Alchemy": using "magic", prayer and meditation to raise our spiritual vibration.

We talk of vibration here in the spiritual sense, but, as I explained in the Introduction (see page 5), our entire being vibrates to a frequency of light and sound. You might have noticed that phrases in our regular speech refer to this energetic vibration. For example, we might refer to a certain topic of conversation as being "heavy" and ask to move on to "lighter" subjects, or we might tell our partner or colleagues to "lighten up" when the conversation becomes a little too "heavy-going". In the same way, every aspect of our energy – our personal vibration – can be sensed by others (more so if they are sensitive), and it is this rate of vibration that we are dealing with here.

In working to raise our vibration, our mind is not always our friend. If we allow it to, it chatters to us like a monkey and will take us way off track by filling our heads with a crowd of unhelpful thoughts that tempt us to deviate from our purpose. And it is our "what if" thoughts that can create heaviness, because they invite fear. Fear makes us static; it paralyses us. When we are too afraid to move away from a toxic situation, it is our thoughts that can literally petrify us. Fear ties us down and becomes a chain, restricting and suppressing us. Allowing fear to get out of control can create mental illness as well as physical disease in our body.

Violet Flame work is very valuable in the process of taming our minds, and especially when used in conjunction with powerful affirmations, known as "decrees". You might like to make up your own or use the following ones, suggested by the New Age visionary and writer Elizabeth Clare Prophet:

> "I AM the boundlessness of the Spirit of Light
> I AM freedom from limitation
> I AM awareness of the Violet Flame
> I AM the living flame of Cosmic Freedom"

Stepping into consciousness

When we shine light on our lives and our selves through personal-development work, as we have been doing in the steps so far, it helps to reflect on our thought processes and readjust our attitudes. Once we literally "lighten up", we become more spiritual and less material. We set ourselves free to be who we really are. Our inner Light becomes visible and we become healthier, happier and noticeably brighter. We shine. What's more, this brightness rubs off on everyone around us. Our own behaviour patterns and the way we deal with others gives our inner Light the opportunity to shine even more brightly. Then, like the ripple effect of a pebble thrown into a pond, the vibration carries into our everyday life. We become a catalyst, an agent of change, just by sharing light in the form of kindness with everyone we meet.

PRACTICE 2
Meditating on the "Violet Flame"

You have already experienced the Violet Flame, in part, in the previous meditation with Archangel Zadkiel (see Practice 1, page 162). The following exercise builds on it by focusing intensely on the violet energy for cleansing, purifying and re-energizing. Keep a pen and your journal nearby to record any feelings, sensations, visions and emotions you have during and after the meditation.

You can also listen again to the download of this exercise at www.AngelLight.co.uk/sevensteps.

1. Sit quietly with your spine straight and feet on the floor. Breathe deeply; slowly filling your lungs and your hara.
2. Before you is a beautiful circle of violet flame. Imagine yourself stepping into it. Feel the energy of the flame rising all around and through you, penetrating and purifying every cell within you. Let the flame dissolve any worries or fears with its beautiful healing light.

3. Imagine that you can feel the violet flame as a warm sensation on the soles of your feet. Visualize the purifying bright colour violet rising through your legs and your body like a soothing warmth.

4. As you breathe in, draw the Violet Flame energy of Zadkiel through you and visualize it cleansing and purifying you as it rises through your abdomen and into your chest. Allow the flame to purify anything "un-loving" you are holding onto in your heart. Release any old memories of painful experiences, any feelings of self-doubt, any self-sabotaging restrictions or barriers you have placed here. Allow the flame to soften and melt away any old negativity in the form of scars you may be holding there. Ask the Violet Flame to cleanse and purify anything it finds that is not pure and true.

5. Now see the flame rising to your neck, cleansing and purifying your throat: your communication centre. Ask Zadkiel's Violet Flame to cleanse and purify any communication with others that may be causing the manifestation of arguments.

6. Ask that all you communicate from now on be pure, truthful and positive expressions of love, always for the highest possible good of all concerned.

7. Now allow the flame to flow down your arms and up into your head at the same time. Here imagine the deep violet flames cleansing, purifying and transmuting all energy in your thoughts. At this point release any old thought patterns you may be holding here that are not yours.

8. Let go of all the energy you have given to other people's opinions and thoughts unnecessarily. Allow the violet flame to purify your thought process to enable you to

immediately discern what is true, letting go of all negative and harmful thoughts and retaining only the positive from this moment on. Hold the violet flame here for a few moments.

9. Now, as the etheric flames of energy rise around you, changing every aspect of negativity within and without, allow yourself to be filled with the joy of the angels.

10. Sense the violet flame all around you. Watch as it becomes deeper and deeper in colour. Repeat any or all of the decrees mentioned earlier. Say them in sets of three, repeating them as much as you like.

11. With a sense of deep gratitude, allow the violet flame to withdraw and, as it fades from your body, down through the soles of your feet, give yourself permission to really feel the difference.

12. Breathing slowly, deeply, deliberately, allow yourself to be back in the present moment. Bring yourself into your own space, your own room, and breathe normally. Feel your body: solid, present and fully grounded. Very slowly, when you're ready, open your eyes.

Wherever you are – on a busy train, in a crowded shopping centre, sitting in a traffic queue – you can transmute feelings of negativity by simply imagining the Violet Flame around you and totally releasing these negative thoughts into it for purification.

Trust that the angelic realms can help you to do this and know that they are delighted to be of assistance. Make a habit of thanking your celestial friends for their help.

Their task is to protect, guide and assist your spiritual growth. Any exercise that you are willing to do that moves you towards spiritual maturity will be supported and celebrated by the heavenly choirs.

To change or not to change: Cosmic Butterfly Soup

Having worked through the five previous steps and nearing the end of what may have been a potentially challenging journey in terms of your personal and spiritual wellbeing, it is time to acknowledge that this really is all about your own transformation. Even if you knew absolutely everything already, by revisiting certain aspects and going deeper you have reinforced change. The angels support your progress. They are willing you to succeed, but they cannot do it for you. They hold you in their light and patiently wait until you feel the transformation taking place and take up the invitation to "fly". I love the following quotation so much; for me it expresses the liberating sensation of overcoming our fear:

> "Come to the edge," he said.
> "We can't, we're afraid!" they responded.
> "Come to the edge," he said.
> "We can't, we will fall!" they responded.
> "Come to the edge," he said.
> And so they came.
> And he pushed them.
> And they flew.
>
> Guillaume Apollinaire

We have, as human beings, the most magnificent and almost incomprehensible design and structure. It is, in fact, so complex that most of us cannot even begin to understand all the science. We are designed to reach our full human potential, to succeed and become the very best we can be: physically (with discipline we can become athletes); mentally (with the right education we have the capacity to be geniuses); and spiritually (some of us do reach a heightened state of being). But, even though we all possess a mind that reasons and free will to make our own choices, not everyone will decide to change. Yet that *potential* for change is in our genes, and not just metaphorically. We *can* transform (if we want to); like magic, metamorphosis can occur.

Look again at the opening quotation from Richard Bach (see page 159). The symbolism of pure joy bursting out of the restrictions of a tight chrysalis, being reborn with strengthened wings and renewed freedom, is just like the feeling of liberation we experience when we grow spiritually.

A brilliant quantum physicist called Dr Elizabet Sahtouris, whose work has been closely documented by Deepak Chopra, wrote about what happens within the life of a caterpillar to show that, in fact, things that look unchangeable are often capable of real transformation.

When a butterfly lays its eggs on a suitable leaf, they hatch and become voracious caterpillars. All they do is eat, consuming everything in their path. When they are completely full, they finally stop eating and spin themselves into a chrysalis, within which a remarkable shift occurs. Dormant cells – called "imaginal" cells – within the body of the caterpillar become active. The immune system sees these cells as external and kills them, but they continue to reactivate. At some stage in this process the caterpillar inside the chrysalis is no more: it has become a liquid-like soup, nothing more than a mush of nutrients. At this point of critical mass these imaginal cells become the new genetic directors of the creature inside the chrysalis and set about organizing everything into a new and beautiful organism. The butterfly takes form, and gradually breaks through the chrysalis – strengthening its wings as it enters the world as a completely different creature.

There is one gene within the caterpillar that allows this metamorphosis to take place, that makes it possible for it to transform into a butterfly, and that same gene is found in only one other place in only one species on the planet: the hearts of human beings.

Can you take in the magnitude of this discovery? Can you even begin to comprehend the human possibilities of change available to us if such a wonderful and mind-boggling transformation takes place within such a tiny beautiful creature?

Just like the caterpillar when it is eating ferociously, we are consuming and digesting a wealth of knowledge and, as we digest it, we gain clarity and wisdom. With guidance, support and practice we are ready to emerge when we finally realize that the "chains" holding us back were our own thoughts, perceptions and illusions. We too are finally free to think and to be whatever our soul desires. I learned about this shared gene almost 20 years ago, just as I was making huge life changes, and the significance of the message remains as true to me today as it did then.

We read the books and do the exercises. We learn spiritual practices such as mindfulness and meditation and we understand how our thoughts affect everything in our world. We do try, don't we? We try very hard, and our desire and commitment in working through this change has not gone unnoticed.

Even if we have got it completely wrong and there are no angels, no higher beings or ascended masters, no high powers of any kind guiding us and no universal energy supporting us, we do know that there is a deeper, innermost mind, a consciousness or Higher Self that yearns for development and longs for change. This aspect of who we are tells us instinctively when the time has come, and generally we cannot resist the power of the inner nudging.

How many times do we expect our lives to improve, for our luck to change with a new car, home, routine, partner, job, dress size?

What we sometimes fail to understand is that knowing something in an intellectual sense is completely different from knowing it emotionally, feeling it physically in the cells of our body. So it is the content and energy of our thoughts, our beliefs and behaviour patterns that we need to change. Only by clearing the negatives, changing the inner life, the spiritual self, will the outer life begin to change. We know this, yet it seems to be one of life's greatest challenges. So often it seems easier to live in blame and fear than in acceptance and love.

So now for the million-dollar question: are you happy to change that negative emotion of blame or fear? (Of course you are... if not, why would you be reading this book?) We are all in the process of change at some level because nothing ever stays the same.

Blame + Negativity = Fear
Acceptance + Positivity = Love

It's good to take stock and reflect on just how far you have come along the journey, and to congratulate yourself for all the time and effort you have put in.

Turning towards joy
The more flame work visualizations we practise, the more relaxed we become and the more chemical wellbeing "drugs" are produced in our bodies.

Four essential chemicals, called neurotransmitters – dopamine, serotonin, oxytocin and endorphins – form the quartet responsible for our happiness and wellbeing. Many situations can trigger these neurotransmitters, but instead of being in the passenger seat, there are ways we can intentionally cause them to flow. They are naturally released into the body when we think positive, happy thoughts, listen to our favourite music, eat our favourite foods, spend time with friends, laugh and have fun... get the picture?

Scientists (and our health practitioners) are becoming more aware of the benefits of positive thinking in relation to mental illnesses such as chronic depression (mindfulness techniques for stress release are regularly recommended), and yet ancient spiritual teachings in the East have been offering these methods for thousands of years. It really is nothing new. We just need reminding to bring it into our conscious awareness and turn towards what gives us joy whenever we can.

The following exercise is similar to "The Audit", which you will find in my friend William Bloom's book *The Endorphin Effect,* which presents a major breakthrough in the field of healthcare and personal development. My version also uses similar methods to those found in NLP (Neuro-Linguistic Programming). Learning NLP is like learning the language of your own mind. It is used as a transformational technique therapy for overcoming phobias and addictions, but also in training the mind to think differently.

In my childhood, the remedy for feeling miserable was to "go out and play", and, inspired by Rodgers and Hammerstein's *The Sound of Music*, this exercise employs the NLP technique of using your "favourite things" to create a "happy anchor", which you can use whenever you need help to transform negativity into joy.

PRACTICE 3
Anchoring your favourite things

Use this simple tool whenever you need to shift your mood from negative to positive. It works because it is extraordinarily difficult for the mind to be in two places at the same time. Take a pen and notebook and write down the answers to the following questions:

1. What is your favourite colour? (It doesn't have to be the colour you look best in!)
2. What is your favourite food? (Peanut butter, broccoli, soy sauce? Pick anything you love!)
3. What is your favourite sound? (It could be birdsong, waves crashing on the shore, a song or piece of music – maybe something you hum along to?)
4. Who is the person that you love to spend time with? (A partner, family member, or a best friend?)
5. What is your favourite smell or fragrance? (Freshly cut grass, roasting coffee beans, your grandmother's perfume?)
6. What is your favourite place to be? (This could be as simple as "curled up on the sofa with my partner/child/cat" or it could be a place you've never been, but have always wanted to visit.)

Once you have the answers written down, continue to the exercise:

1. Imagine you are in your favourite place, or a place you long to go, with your favourite person in the whole world, eating your all-time favourite food. You can smell the

most delightful fragrances and hear all your favourite sounds. Bliss. Can you really engage with it and sense how it makes you feel?

2. Breathe that feeling deep down into your belly and hold it there for a few moments, allowing yourself to really enjoy the sensations.

3. Now think of your favourite colour and imagine Archangel Zadkiel sending angels to bless you. Sense a beautiful, loving warm mist surrounding you in that happy sensation.

4. Next, think of a name to call this sensation (you might call it Zadkiel but it can be anything at all that makes you feel happy). As you pinch your finger and thumb on your right hand together tightly, say this word to yourself three times and then open your eyes and release your fingers.

5. Take a couple of normal, relaxed breaths and then try it again. Close your eyes and pinch your finger and thumb while thinking of the colour you chose and saying the name you gave the technique (out loud works best). This is now your "happy anchor".

I've been teaching this "happy thoughts" exercise as a tool for raising endorphins for a long time and the consensus is that it really works.

If producing endorphins soothes physical pain and makes you happy then clearly the reverse is also true. If you suppress these neurotransmitters you will find lifting the dark mood extremely difficult. Negative self-talk is sometimes so automatic that you are unaware of it. Following an argument or a disappointment, do you go over and over the details in your head as if pressing an invisible "rewind" button? (Yes,

I'm sure we all do that.) Buddhist teaching explains that this attachment to our thoughts is part of the human condition that creates suffering. We can literally talk ourselves into a dark place of sheer misery.

If you can catch yourself having negative or toxic thoughts, stop yourself and ask whether you are happy in this place, or whether you would like to be somewhere else. If you'd like to change your thoughts, then you can. With practice, it becomes an almost instant transformation.

CAUTION: CHANGE AHEAD

Personal transformation at this level of spiritual development can be life changing, but also very challenging for those around you and so requires a warning.

Be aware that your transformation is personal to you. You can guide by example but you can't take passengers, and this might mean losing a few people on the way. Be very sure that even if they don't cast you adrift they might not like the "new you" as much as the old one. Rather than be happy for you one or two people might be jealous or feel rejected because they cannot keep up with your pace. Friends might struggle to keep up or judge and criticize your new spiritual practices or choices. All we can do is remain true to what feels right in our own heart, and practice the art of forgiveness.

Transmuting blame to love

As we learned in Step 5, when we looked at the ancient Huna practice of *Ho'oponopono* (see Practice 4, page 150), loving and forgiving go hand in hand.

Forgiveness of self and others is clearly a vital part of spiritual growth, yet both can be so very difficult to do. Many of my clients will explain all the reasons why they can "never forgive" a certain person in their lives. Whether it is an ancient wound or still fresh and raw, the memory of abuse, abandonment, betrayal or rejection is just too painful. What they don't realise is that, by hanging on to that hurt and anger, they are creating a hardened area in the heart, a dark hole in their psyche (and aura) and potentially a disease that their body then has to repair.

As well as feelings about others, we can also hold on to emotions, such as shame or guilt, that are directed entirely towards our selves. In this case it is our own actions, thoughts or behaviour that we are unable to forgive.

Yet, when we do eventually forgive – whoever it is – a renewed sense of freedom occurs, and a lightness is created that softens the heart, fills the black hole and heals the disease. It is a spiritual act of such high value that it is truly Divine. It sets us free, releases the etheric chains we create for ourselves and raises our vibration beyond measure.

So, how do we forgive ourselves when there seems no hope? How is it possible to forgive someone when we believe they have all but ruined our life? My advice is to call upon Archangel Zadkiel (and any of the others you have worked with along your journey) to help you with forgiveness. Remember: the person you are unable to forgive also has a spark of the Divine within them. They have a soul, and though the light within it may have been dimmed, it is still there, even if we can't see it. Can you forgive that speck of light, as if it was the smallest of diamonds hiding in the shadows? Once, this person was a newborn – a beautiful, harmless, vulnerable little soul who had not and could not possibly hurt you. As the baby grew into a child with absolutely no intention of causing pain to anyone, the light shone brightly within. Over time, however, life and circumstances have instilled within this innocent an internal pain, which was never expressed, and so the light became dimmed. Could you forgive that child? If so, marvellous – if you can take this first step, your powers of forgiveness, like any other muscle, will surely grow from strength to strength

PRACTICE 4
Tuning into Zadkiel's energy for forgiveness

Call to mind someone or something that you can't forgive, and use the following practice daily until you have transmuted blame to love and forgiveness. Repeat this exercise for each person and everything you need to forgive until there is no blame left in your heart.

1. Bathe your senses in the Violet Flame (as described in Practice 1, page 162).
2. When you feel grounded and in a calm space, bring the action or the person to mind and observe your feelings about them/it without allowing your thoughts and mind to engage in the drama.

If we harbour thoughts of spite or vengeance, hoping and wishing that those who have harmed us will in some way get their just desserts, it creates more negativity inside our own hearts. We actually add our own energy to the existing pain, which only serves to amplify it. We don't have to like the person who has harmed us, and we certainly don't have to condone their actions, but if we can just relax on the judgement, changing our focus from negative to positive by wishing them no harm, it is a great beginning. Our negative thoughts transform into positive energy and this act of letting go becomes one of loving-kindness, a way of weaving a Golden Thread of Love into our everyday life in a practical and helpful way.

Letting go

There is a great freedom in letting go of judgement and fear. To allow others the freedom to make their own decisions, their own mistakes, only giving advice when asked, is an act of loving-kindness and wisdom. Those who judge others harshly are usually incredibly hard on themselves too, often holding themselves and others to extraordinarily unrealistic standards, all the while totally unaware of how harmful this behaviour can be. And, truthfully, that's not really being loving! We are all a work in progress, and truly letting go takes dedication, self-discipline and focus. When we call in and work with Zadkiel, we learn to let others be who they are, and our relaxed and positive attitude is reflected in how we feel towards everyone, including ourselves. Engaging with the power of the angels heightens our awareness, too, and so progress is much faster. This transformation, however long it takes, results in making us happier, more loving in nature, more accepting of our own qualities, and "lighter" in the process.

PRACTICE 5
Engaging with loving-kindness on a daily basis

The Buddhist practice of *metta bhavana*, meaning "loving-kindness", is also helpful in taking forgiveness to the next level. This exercise makes for a perfect daily practice, as it teaches us how to send friendliness and harmlessness around the world – even to those that we have had to work hard to forgive.

If you need to refresh your memory about using the guided meditations, see Tools for Your Journey (page 17).

1. Before getting comfortable, light a candle and spend a few minutes breathing deeply in the light before closing your eyes.

2. Continue to breathe deeply, filling your lower abdomen with the breath and releasing slowly, allowing your body to fully relax.

3. Focus on the flame of a candle if your eyes open, or, if they are closed, on the space behind your eyes. Concentrate on your breath passing in through your nose, following it all the way down to the hara and allow any thoughts that are not about your breath to drift away, telling yourself you can think about that later.

4. Start the "loving-kindness" process by thinking of someone you don't know well – someone in passing, such as the owner of the local shop, or your child's teacher, for example. Send kind thoughts to them, wishing them well, similar to wishing someone a "happy holiday".

5. Now think of someone you like and know well. Send kind thoughts to them in the same way.

6. Next, think of someone who annoys you. Send them kind thoughts of wellbeing and friendliness, such as: "I wish you well" (even though they are not your favourite person, you can wish them no harm).

7. Now bring a more challenging person to mind, someone with whom you have a real problem. Can you wish them well? If not, don't worry; just try to wish them no harm.

8. Let the difficult person go and now think of someone you really care about. Wish them friendly thoughts of love and kindness.

9. Send that loving thought to everyone in your town or village, whether you know them or not, and spread the empathic feeling of kindness to everyone living there. Now spread it to your whole country, then continent, and then gradually imagine weaving loving-kindness all the way around the world.

10. Breathing slowly, deeply, deliberately, allow yourself to be back in the present moment. Bring yourself into your own space, your own room, and breathe normally. Feel your body: solid, present and fully grounded. Very slowly, when you're ready, open your eyes.

Transformation takes time

Some of the concepts of transformation in Step 6 are truly life changing, but transformation doesn't happen overnight. Sometimes it's not always possible to immediately forgive (or even want to forgive) someone who has badly hurt you. Some people hold on to a desire for revenge, while others simply resolve never to forget the crime. If you find at this time you are not ready to let go and forgive, please don't feel in any way a failure. Don't be hard on yourself and add to the guilt.

Even those of us who think we have forgiven someone might catch ourselves retelling the same story – which is always a hint that forgiveness hasn't fully taken effect. It can take a lifetime, or sometimes many, to fully release those powerful emotions and learn to finally let them go. Our emotional body can be compared to the layers of an onion, which need to be unpeeled one at a time. The point is to see the value of forgiveness and how it can aid our personal and spiritual growth, and then strive towards it as fearlessly as we can.

The angels are here to help and support you, however long it may take.

DAILY PRAYER

Dear Archangel Zadkiel,

May I step into your Light.

I thank you for your purity and power.

Enfold me in your violet light and give me the gift of pure joy in my heart.

May I always see the best in every situation, offering positive enthusiasm, mercy and compassion wherever I am.

May I too serve as a messenger of freedom and light.

Thank you.

Amen.

STEP 7

PUT LOVE INTO ACTION
FINDING PEACE WITH ARCHANGEL URIEL

"Avoiding danger is no safer in the long run than outright exposure. Life is either a daring adventure, or nothing."

Helen Keller

ANGEL ASSOCIATIONS

Attributes: Peace, Ministry, Devotional Worship,
    Earth, Support, Peace, Spiritual Empowerment
Colour: Keeper of the gold and ruby-red flame
Planetary influence: Earth
Crystal: Ruby
Day of the week: Friday
Ashram: Tatra Mountains, Poland

I believe we are *all* called to serve a higher purpose, and just as we are all unique individuals, we will serve in our own way. So how do we use our spirituality to wholeheartedly serve the greater good? Will *you* commit to world peace and put love into action with authenticity and integrity? To do so involves self-discipline and constant practice, so Step 7 focuses on self-reflection and various spiritual practices that you can adapt to everyday life in practical ways.

The great angelic messenger Uriel brings peace by calling on each of us to serve as a Spiritual Warrior (or Light Worker, Earth Angel – whatever name we choose to represent the action of fully embodying our spiritual nature). This is the step where the brilliance and illumination of Uriel's Light highlights our attributes and enables us to decide how we can put our spiritual strengths into action. You can best do this by taking some time to deeply reflect on your work so far. Then decide which of the spiritual practices you have learned in this book you wish to take into your everyday spiritual practice to continue making a difference to your life, and the world. The practical exercises in this step will help you to:

- Connect with and experience inner peace and serenity.
- Make peace with your past and bring that attitude into your wider world.
- Gain support in choosing the right spiritual practice for you, so that you begin to shine your Light into the world in service of others.
- Get clear on your intentions so that you are aware of why you are doing things, and let go of any practices or relationships that don't serve you.

Stepping into Archangel Uriel's Light

Uriel's name has been translated as both the "fire of God" and the "face of God", but either way he is said to be one of the great four "Angels of the Presence" alongside Michael, the leader of all the hosts of angel warriors who battle against the dark side. Archangel Uriel is also the Angel of Salvation, who is reputed to be the powerful cherubim who stands guard at the gates of the Garden of Eden as well as the gates to Hell. However, unlike the armour-clad representation of Michael with his breastplate, sword and shield, Uriel's armour is that of serenity and peace.

He is the Archangel who, when we buckle under pressure, gives us our "spiritual backbone". When I teach people how to engage with this angelic presence in my workshops, they often experience an energy of incredible calmness and inner strength. And it is this quality he brings to the whole of humanity. Uriel is the angelic presence that teaches us that the greatest leadership comes from peace within, and it is this *inner* peace that will create peace in the wider world.

You can also ask Uriel, just as you can all the angels, to help you to heal and support your own physical health and wellbeing. Uriel will help you to strengthen the bones of your support system – your skeleton and, in particular, your spine. When you feel unsure about stepping in and helping someone in trouble, it is Uriel who will give you the inner strength to stand up for yourself and others.

PRACTICE 1
Feeling the peace within with Uriel

Perhaps the one thing we long for most in our lives, and in the wider world, is peace. This meditation can help you connect with Uriel to bring more serenity and calm.

If you need to refresh your memory about using the guided meditations, see Tools for Your Journey (page 17), or, if you prefer to listen to it as a download, go to: www.AngelLight. co.uk/sevensteps.

1. Sitting comfortably in your own quiet place, with your back straight and hands resting on your lap, open, facing upwards, begin to breathe slowly and deeply.

2. Either aloud or in your mind call to Archangel Uriel and the angels of Peace (three times): "Archangel Uriel, may I step into your Light."

3. Imagine that around you is a deep red light, and that within it there is a bright, rich circle of gold that gleams and shines as it slowly spins at ground level, rising and turning around your body until it reaches above your head, before coming down again slowly and resting at heart level. See the light as it swirls around you, embracing and protecting you.

4. Call out to the angels of Uriel and ask them to come close to you now. Feel the warmth of their love surrounding you as they approach and enter your auric field of energy.

5. Visualize the beautiful, rich ruby-red colour before your eyes and call upon the mighty presence of Archangel Uriel. In this presence, accept and allow yourself to feel the peace within your body. Let go now of all tension in your muscles and feel the presence of peace in your feet, legs, hips, back, stomach, chest, shoulders, down your arms and in your hands, up through your neck and into your face, head and scalp.

6. Allowing yourself to feel completely relaxed, now visualize the golden circle shining as stars before you. Imagine that you can hear the gentle music of the spheres ringing in your ears. You may even feel a tingling of the scalp and an opening of the third eye. Your body and your senses are harmonizing with the Universe.

7. You are connecting with the universal energy of Divine peace; the peace that surpasses all understanding. If you feel you would like to offer yourself in service to universal peace, do this now by saying, "Archangel Uriel and the angels of peace, I am ready to be at peace. I am ready to

feel peace in my body, peace in my mind, peace in my heart, peace in my spirit, peace in my soul. I offer myself now as a channel of peace. Use me, as a messenger of Divine peace."

8. Now, breathing in the beautiful rich red light that surrounds you, sense the gentle slow movement of the golden light once again as it moves around your body – first passing down to your feet as if melding with the Earth's energies, then rising slowly up your body, strengthening your spine as it rises, giving you purpose and fortitude, stamina and stability. The golden circle of light rises high above your head as you watch it in your mind's eye. It passes through the ceiling, the roof, out into the sky and rises upwards. Watch it in your imagination as it moves slowly through the clouds and upwards towards the stars.

9. Imagine yourself now floating with the circle of golden light, surrounded and supported by the angels of peace. The golden circle has formed a beautiful gold bubble of light. You and the angels take positions around it and pull, bursting the bubble and sending sparkles of golden loving peace back down towards the earth, landing wherever you feel peace and love are needed. As the angels escort you back down to where you are now sitting, you feel energized, strong, safe, fully supported by the Universe, the Divine and the angels. You feel totally and completely at peace.

10. Breathing slowly, deeply, deliberately, allow yourself to be back in the present moment. Bring yourself into your own space, your own room, and breathe normally. Feel your body: solid, present and fully grounded. Very slowly, when you're ready, open your eyes.

Sending your Light into the world

Uriel's role of guardian of the Earth links him to the element of earth, too, and as you work with his Light you may develop a much deeper desire to work actively towards world peace in some way. You might not be motivated by politics but called to work with environmental groups like Greenpeace or similar worthwhile causes and charities. Or, you might simply develop a great love of everything about Mother Nature and the planet, in which case spending more time gardening, bee-keeping, or any other ways of working in nature will help you to tap into this calming, grounding energy.

Uriel's energy will certainly encourage you to be kind and peaceful in all your dealings. It will also enable you to balance the internal battle between yin and yang or feminine and masculine energies. This means that if you are feeling particularly vulnerable and weak – or the opposite: rather too strident and aggressive – you can call upon Uriel to bring balance, serenity and peace of mind.

You might like to stop for a moment to reflect upon how you would like to connect more deeply with the Archangel Uriel in a personal way, following your own natural spiritual rhythm and intuition, to bring greater peace to your life and the planet.

Creating a conscious daily practice

It is one thing to intellectualize ideas – reading books, going to workshops and absorbing the basic teachings and holding it all in your "head-space" – but quite another to put them all into daily practice. To be fully conscious and mindful of our thoughts, the words we speak and the actions we take, is hard work. It means practising *all the time*. Note: this doesn't mean you'll get it *right* all the time. I doubt that anyone can do this, and even the very best of us fall short of perfection.

Such constant practice is still necessary, however, because, as I've said before, *energy follows thought*. If you have reached this point in your personal journey, you'll be starting to see that *everything* you put into words and actions contains the energy of whatever you are thinking at the time. For example, when you're asked to do something that gives you pleasure, you're likely to put joyful energy into it – love flows into the action. Similarly, if you dislike the task, or the person asking you to do it, the same thing will happen, except this time resentment flows into the action; there is no love in the gesture at all. Understanding this flow of energy and becoming aware of your own thoughts, becoming mindful as you help others or carry out your daily chores – this is what's meant by spiritual awareness.

You can start to inject this into your everyday actions by first becoming aware of the intentions behind them. So, before cooking a meal, you might think of the nourishment it will bring to you and your family. Similarly, if you dislike a task, try to say "no" to it. A simple phrase like: "I'm sorry, but right now I don't have the energy for that..." can be all it takes to avoid carrying out the task with resentment. Being truthful about your needs and intention rarely offends. It is expressing your own truth unkindly, without any necessary explanations, that can cause hurt and disconnection.

Step into spiritual empowerment

The opportunity for personal spiritual empowerment and fulfillment is right now. We are being called in greater numbers to be Light Workers on a grand scale. While fearful news events, wars and strange weather patterns might be enough for some to conclude that the darker side of our world seems to be taking control, inducing fear into many hearts and minds, on the opposing side of such dark forces is an army of Spiritual Warriors, a host of Light Workers, who are spreading love and peace.

A Course In Miracles (often referred to as ACIM or "the Course"), channelled by Helen Schucman, offers a curriculum to bring about "spiritual transformation", but its most important teaching is that we can have only fear or love, but not both at the same time.

When love and joy fills our soul, then fear disappears from our hearts. Of course, it is quite normal to feel fearful or unsure sometimes, but it is how we handle that fear, what we do with it, that counts.

When we are called to serve the Light, angels surround us, inspire and protect us, bringing gifts of renewed energy and healing or new supportive, like-minded friends into our lives. Whether we recognize the presence of our angelic helpers or not, they enfold us in invisible wings of love and support. We have to learn to allow ourselves to be open to this. Strange, sometimes unnerving coincidences might seem unreal. Beautiful visions in nature such as rainbows, prominent stars or sky formations catch our attention. To some, these are simply examples of the beauty of nature; to others they are signs of a deep connection with all that is. No matter what is going on around us, in our own lives or the wider world, we may always try to see the positive and feel love for others. But we can't just sit back and wait. We have to be proactive. Use the following affirmation to support you:

I offer the best of who I am, in service for the highest good.

Peace starts within each one of us

It is a fact that we can only ever have world peace when each of us discovers inner peace and puts that peace into action. When we deal with everyone, ourselves included, with respect and compassion; when we live consciously, aware that our actions affect everyone else too, then world peace could indeed start in our own kitchen!

Inner peace for your heart and soul may be what you are craving. Or, if you live in conflict, maybe it's peace within your family or relationships you need. All this can be requested, and found, when you follow the previous six steps and then tune into the amazing energy of Archangel Uriel's Light. By asking him to enable you to become a channel for the Divine's vision of peace, Uriel and the angels of peace will work with you and through you.

Life so often challenges us and we can become weary, confused and exhausted by the pain we've inflicted upon ourselves emotionally through mental turmoil. Our despair or even sometimes the physical torment of illness, as I've already discussed, can be brought about by our own inability to connect with the Divine forces of healing and forgiveness, which are always available to us. And to be at peace internally when all about us are seemingly contriving to create chaos and stress is nigh on impossible at times! All the ancient teachings through the ages advise that we can only be happy and at peace with the world when we learn to *be still* – which is perhaps one of the greatest tests of being human.

One of the surest ways of finding the peace we seek is to open our hearts to become truly peaceful. We will then be at liberty to assist others. Simply call to the great Archangel Uriel and the angels of peace, in your own words as well as those found here, making sure you speak from the heart, with true ardency and purity of intent.

PRACTICE 2
Working with the angels for peace

Here is another meditative practice for accepting the gift of inner peace and asking to be used as a channel of Divine peace.

To do this, set your intention to release any feelings of anxiety that you hold towards yourself and others. It is wise to make sure you've completed the previous practices to connect with, acknowledge and release old wounds and painful memories from the past. They are unwanted in the role of "peace-maker".

If you need to refresh your memory about using the guided meditations, see Tools for Your Journey (page 17), or, if you prefer to listen to a similar meditation as a download, go to: www.AngelLight.co.uk/sevensteps.

1. Sit comfortably in your own quiet place, making sure your spine is straight. Give this meditative exercise a deeper, more prayerful intention by starting with your hands crossed over your heart, then letting them gently fall until they are resting on your lap, facing upwards.
2. Breathe in deeply, without raising your shoulders, and as you exhale release the tension from your neck and shoulders, allowing them to drop. (We often wonder why we have aches and pains, perhaps headaches, yet fail to recognize the tension that we carry within our own body, particularly in the neck.)
3. Visualize your concerns being blown away and dissolved in a bright, loving light.

4. Repeat this slow rhythmic breathing in and out, releasing tension from all the muscles of your body, all the way from the soles of your feet to your scalp, until you feel relaxed and calm.

5. Breathe in deeply and, with meaning, say to yourself: "*Peace*, be still" three times, emphasizing the first word. Now repeat the phrase, again three times, this time emphasizing the next word: "Peace, *be* still." Finally, repeat with emphasis on the final word: "Peace, be *still*." Do this in groups of three as many times as it takes for you to really feel the word "peace" resonating through your body.

6. Now, when you are ready, call Archangel Uriel by name. If you feel comfortable, calling the name gently out loud will give the exercise greater effect (your voice adds power to the intention). If this doesn't feel comfortable, don't get anxious, simply stay with your own feelings until you become more confident. Now say the following three times (if it resonates with you): "*Archangel Uriel and the angels of peace. I am ready to accept the gift of peace. I love peace. I AM peaceful. I AM at peace. I AM a peaceful being, and I share peace with others. Use me as an instrument of Divine peace.*"

7. Sitting and breathing slowly, give yourself a few moments with this powerful affirmation, really allowing it to settle into your whole being.

8. Breathing slowly, deeply, deliberately, allow yourself to be back in the present moment. Bring yourself into your own space, your own room, and breathe normally. Feel your body: solid, present and fully grounded. Very slowly, when you're ready, open your eyes.

The Golden Thread

Let's recap and reflect on the Golden Thread of Light that has led us to this place, and how the Seven Steps we've explored come together to bring inner peace, peace in our lives and families, and perhaps even that seemingly elusive world peace.

1. Communication and awakening (Gabriel)

Agreement can't ever be achieved unless dialogue takes place. Being able to discuss issues, cooperate with others and move towards understanding are at the foundation of creating peace. Sometimes it can be difficult to enter or engage in these kinds of conversations, especially with those who have hurt us, but if we want to heal ourselves and/or the situation it is essential to open the channels of communication – and to keep them open.

Working with the angels will strengthen our communication skills by deepening our understanding of others. If we are having difficulty communicating with someone, we can first start by intensifying our own inner Light. Call upon Archangel Gabriel to help by sending the light forward into an anticipated positive outcome. Watching out for signs, ask Gabriel to nudge us into being in the right place at the right time to enable it to happen. Invite the angels of communication to inspire us and reveal to us the perfect words and methods, prompting us to speak when the time is right.

Create an affirmation and repeat it often, such as:

I connect with the oneness of all creation focusing on the best outcome for all, as I communicate from the heart, spreading love and peace.

2. Wisdom (Jophiel)

By becoming aware of our own spiritual beliefs and respecting others', we start to see that we have more similarities than differences. All the major world religions have the same tenets at their heart and teach that the more we develop our spirituality, quickening our step along the path to contentment, the more we learn to turn towards love. Mutual respect for others is not a sign of failure or capitulation, but rather a willingness to see the good in others and understand how they feel. Once we have gained this insight and level of heightened understanding, it still takes strength and willpower to stand back and let go of the need to impose our "better" ways on others.

All of us are part of the vast network of energy that connects humanity to the rest of the Universe. The Angel of Illumination urges us to recognize the interconnection by radiating positive, peaceful energy of tolerance and respect to all.

Create an affirmation and repeat it often, such as:

Radiating my Light I connect with universal wisdom and trusting my inner wisdom I am at one with my family, and all of humanity.

3. Protection (Michael)

In order to enjoy peace of mind, we need to feel safe and secure. Taking steps to protect our self is an act of self-care, and at the same time holding strong boundaries protects those in our care. By offering fair and impartial judgement when there is conflict, we create an environment in which others can begin their own steps towards peace. We don't have to be strident or imposing like the Archangel Michael depicted in art, and not all of us have to be outspoken. By raising our awareness of how we best operate within the realms of our own personality, our relationships, environment and the world around us, we can come to accept responsibility for our part in co-creating our world. We can't all don the physical armour of battle, but we can develop an inner strength and radiance that enables us to conduct our life in a confident manner. This creates an energy of strength and calm around us where people may feel safe in our presence. When we are shining our inner Light as brightly as we can, we automatically empower others to do the same.

Create an affirmation and repeat it often, such as:

I confidently shine my Divine Light, knowing that I am strong, honest and safe.

4. Healing (Raphael)

When we begin to understand that our ailments and illnesses are often due to negative emotional disturbances, such as stress and anxiety, we start to see the importance of protecting and caring for our Light. Our daily practices are helpful in keeping us on track, but how we show up in life and how we express our Light are equally so. Dis-ease arises when we dim down the light in our cells, as this damages them, so we need to change the way we react to the busyness of life in order to stay grounded and peaceful and to shine our Light as brightly as possible. And this means taking responsibility for our own self-care.

Create an affirmation and repeat it often, such as:

I am healed, as I lovingly take responsibility for my thoughts, words and actions. Healing Angel Light flows through every cell of my body.

5. Love (Chamuel)

When we choose to heal our minds and bodies of past hurts and transgressions against us, we bring love back into our life and begin the challenging process of forgiveness and reconciliation. This is, perhaps, the hardest part of creating peace, because it requires not only putting the pain and hurt to one side (ideally forgotten permanently) but often there will be the need for us to heal our own sense of failure too, as low self-esteem and lack of self-love can keep us stuck.

Create an affirmation and repeat it often, such as:

I graciously forgive all past hurtful situations, including those towards myself, knowing that love will fill that space as I release them into the Light.

6. Transformation (Zadkiel)

By holding onto bitterness we only harm ourselves, as we now know that it is the energy of our own thoughts that causes emotional imbalance, leading to unhappiness and potential disease of the mind and body. Compassion and forgiveness cannot only improve quality of life and the environment but will lead to a greater sense of contentment and heightened, lasting joy. Call on the angels to help us transform all negative thought into positive energy, turning away from fear towards joy.

Create an affirmation and repeat it often, such as:

I attract only loving people and helpful situations into my life. I freely step forwards, confidently, with joy in my heart.

7. Peace (Uriel)

Using meditative practices for attaining inner peace, we will move towards "outer" peace with others. How can we possibly not? Creating and maintaining balance and harmony in ourselves – being "still" – is necessary through reflection, contemplation and meditation. Personal forgiveness and the inner harmony that is achieved will be reflected in the actions we take in dealing with others. Not only is this a balanced approach to relationships but it also reflects in the health and wellbeing of our own body. Harmony and peace is essential in healing, and good medicine for the body, mind and soul.

Create an affirmation and repeat it often, such as:

I love peace, I am peace, I live peace.

PRACTICE 3
Taking seven steps towards peace

This exercise can be used at every level and is designed to reinforce your own values and remind you how you have developed, specifically in relation to peace.

Using your journal, make notes of how you could include each of the Seven Steps in encouraging peace in the following places:

- Personally: for your self, and between family and friends.
- Locally: in the community, at work and through supporting others.
- Environmentally: for the good of the planet.

- Nationally: by supporting others and promoting peace, compassion, tolerance and understanding.
- Inter-culturally: by continually learning about other cultures, religions and people, to gain a greater understanding of their beliefs, fears and goals.
- Internationally: by supporting and encouraging the politicians and leaders that work on programmes for resolving global conflict.

Stepping into your Spiritual Warrior Light

I think we have established that change is exceedingly difficult for us – we all feel safety in the security of what we know. Having worked with the transmutational energy of Archangel Zadkiel in Step 6, you will probably already have noticed that you feel different. Uriel calls you for greater and bigger things, but by tuning into your own soul's calling you will undoubtedly feel happiest doing whatever you can, in your own way.

Are you prepared to take a risk or two for the things that you really hold dear, that make your heart sing?

Very often it is the fears and vulnerabilities of those around us that prevent us from following the path we wish to tread. On the one hand, we fear that we'll upset the equilibrium; on the other, we fear that our Light will never get a chance to shine.

At some point in the future, you are going to look back on all the things you wanted to do with your life and either say "I did it!" or "I wish I had..." If the first statement is the one you want to make, there's no time like the present for making those words come true.

If you choose the latter, however, you need do nothing. Wishing is free. Everything else comes with a price.

So, is it not the case that a Spiritual Warrior/Light Worker simply has to be "nice" to everyone? I would suggest that perhaps "niceness" doesn't quite hit the spot... First, therefore, we should clarify what it means to be a Spiritual Warrior, or, rather, what it does *not* mean.

A Spiritual Warrior/Light Worker is not someone prepared to do anything for the sake of a peaceful life.

Neither is it someone who has their head so high in the clouds that the slightest change of airflow can knock them sideways.

It is not a person who believes everything he/she is told – a gullible soul steeped in superstition, following new rules and old without questioning their personal value, validity or authenticity.

It is definitely not someone who has read hundreds of spiritual books, but without implementing any of the wisdom found within the pages.

It is not a person unable to control his/her own emotions and express them in a calm, intelligent manner.

It is not someone who imposes her/his beliefs on others with little regard, respect or knowledge of their negative impact, or the consequences.

So what *does* it mean to be a Light Worker, a Spiritual Warrior?

I would say it is a person who truly believes in love and compassion, humility, honour, respect and reason, truth, justice, faith, prayer, change, empowerment and purpose, and tries hard to put these things into practice. They don't need to create a tidal wave all on their own, but even small steps to bring harmony, peace and love, taken as often as they can, will, when taken together, make a noticeable difference.

A Light Worker/Spiritual Warrior is someone who is capable of warmly greeting others, able to welcome and embrace difference. They will be able to hold an opinion in conversation lightly, see the humour in situations and laugh at themselves, aware of the tricks the ego can play.

Is a Light Worker/Spiritual Warrior someone prepared to serve others without counting any cost to self? A tricky question, as we all need to have a sense of value; indeed, it's a human requirement. The angels exist to serve the Divine and humanity. There is no greater cause. Selfless acts come from the heart, with a genuine desire to serve. Angels do not have ego but we must always offer our thanks for their help. My understanding is that it is with gratitude that they receive praise and acknowledgement for their constant support and assistance. It is an exchange of energy, of mutual appreciation. Just as we too in our humanness flourish on gratitude, acceptance and love. This is the essence of value.

Service vs self-care

Many people today view service as a throwback to the days of subordination or control, oppression and manipulation. It may seem a sweeping generalization, but it seems to me we are nowadays encouraged to put ourselves and our own needs first, as opposed to working for the greater good. Of course, we need to see to our own welfare. If we are over-stretched and tired, often because we have not developed the skill of saying "no", we run out of steam. Tiredness leads to the inability to cope with stress, we then lose our ability to focus clearly and are not much use to anyone!

But there is an important difference between self-care and selfishness. The term "self-centred" can have more than one meaning too: namely, that we need to learn how to be more centred in *self*. That means being fully grounded, focused and strong in the knowledge of the unique and Divine self, understanding who and what we are.

We also need to understand our limitations and confidently use our talents. However, when the whole Universe begins to spin around our own wants and needs in a sense of false self-importance then we have become self-centred, more undeniably selfish and a slave to ego, rather than servant of the Divine.

Nevertheless, it does not benefit us in any way to become the object of manipulation and bullying, and we should never allow this kind of abusive behaviour to happen to us, or anyone around us. Offering help in the form of respectful service to those with good intentions or those who have suffered misfortune or require help in order to achieve their valuable goals is sound, empowering and to be actively encouraged.

We all know what is needed within our family, but what about taking steps to become involved with the wider community, or even political or planetary issues? If you already care for children, why not train and help as a volunteer with an organization such as Childline, an afterschool club or association such as Brownies, Scouts or Guides? If you deeply care about loneliness and mental health issues, you could volunteer with the Samaritans. Or assist the emergency services by training to become a first responder. If you love animals, you might like to become a dog-walker or pet-sitter. And if you feel passionate about politics, then you might want to join your local party or sign up as a volunteer for an environmental group helping to serve the planet.

If your life already involves a large degree of serving, in your family or through other commitments, you might sometimes feel unappreciated or undervalued. If you ever feel like this, please just stop for a moment and consider how many lives you have touched with your kindness. Ask the angels to revitalize your sense of purpose and you will find that your energy and enthusiam will return.

Remember that the angels are around you to support and encourage. The more you feel a sense of loving gratitude and offer to work with them, the more you will sense their presence assisting you in return. As Florence Scovel Shinn said:

> "The game of life is a game of boomerangs. Our thoughts, deeds and words return to us sooner or later with astounding accuracy."

When we begin to comprehend that what we are sending out is going to return to us, whether we like it or not, then making the effort to live by the universal laws daily and putting love into action really, really, really starts to make sense.

May that which you send forth daily create most glorious tomorrows.

DAILY PRAYER

Dear Archangel Uriel,

I am willing to fulfil my purpose now, whatever that might be.

I ask for your help in strengthening my resolve, in standing up for what is right. As I let go of all aspects of fear, I ask that I may step fully into your radiant Light and be the Spiritual Warrior I was meant to be, in whatever way I may serve best.

Enable me to be at peace in my mind, heart, body and soul.

Empower me to assist the Universe and angels as an agent of change.

I am ready to be of service.

Use me as a channel of Divine Light.

Thank you.

Amen.

SEVEN MORE STEPS...

CONTINUING YOUR JOURNEY INTO THE LIGHT

"Look for the light. Look for it in everything. Look for it in yourself, in your children, in your job, and in your dreams. Look for it in the food you eat and in the people you surround yourself with."

Debbie Ford

I hope that the Seven Steps have given you the encouragement to start your own spiritual journey. The framework of Seven Steps has been a powerful method that I have used and taught to my workshop participants and course students for many years, with amazing results. But, in truth, YOUR Seven Steps may be different from mine. Indeed, there may be many others that will carry you forwards on your personal journey.

For now, here are seven more steps that you may like to consider:

1. Practise daily affirmations

One of the simplest ways of reinforcing the power of Divine energy in your soul is to repeat a daily affirmation, ideally three times, each morning and evening. You will have read many during your time on this journey with me, and will find many more affirmations online, but you can also receive a weekly affirmation from me every Monday morning. Just sign up for them at the website below or follow me on Facebook or Twitter.

2. Maintain open lines of communication with the Divine

Meditate and reflect daily on your spiritual connection. You may find it hard at first, but with patience and practice it will become easier. You can join my community of like-minded souls and download guided meditations with all of the seven Archangels in this book. Just go to: www.AngelLight.co.uk/sevensteps.

3. Practise techniques for grounding and protection

We are bombarded by negativity every day. Ensure you protect yourself from the moment you awaken each morning using the ideas in Step 3, or create your own.

4. Explore healing techniques

Healing takes many forms, from simple relaxation techniques to improve mind and body, to more advanced body healing. Explore those techniques you feel called to, and seek to work on both physical and mental issues you may have. Don't forget to consult with qualified therapists and/or medical professionals if necessary for support along the way.

5. Join a local meditation or reflection group

Sharing and working with others over tea or coffee will enable you to discover greater insights and feel connected to the world. If you cannot find a local group, ask for an invitation to my Facebook group, "Educating Heart & Soul", where you can contact other readers and develop spiritual relationships and soul-companions in your own area.

6. Never stop learning

Growth and transformation come from continually learning more about yourself and the world around you. Read books, watch positive, informative videos, study new ideas and share your experiences. If you'd like to gain a greater depth of understanding about the Seven Steps I teach, enrol on my home study programme, Educating Heart & Soul (there's a special discounted offer online just for reading this book!).

7. Explore your life purpose

Each of us is called to serve, sometimes just by "Be-ing" our true self. Your calling may be to your family and local community. Or you may be called to a greater purpose. Whatever level it may be, find your passion and follow it, for when you are passionate about helping others, you really are stepping up towards a personal state of higher purpose.

Join our community of seekers to receive wisdom, to learn and to share our spiritual journeys together. Just sign up for free at www.AngelLight.co.uk/sevensteps, or follow me on Facebook.

CONCLUSION

LIVING IN THE LIGHT

"Light gives of itself freely, filling all available space. It does not seek anything in return; it asks not whether you are friend or foe. It gives of itself and is not thereby diminished."

Michael Strassfeld

I spend much of my time travelling around the UK and other parts of the world, running workshops and retreats. And among all this lovable work I enjoy a wonderful involvement as much as possible with my friends, family and grandchildren, and I have lots of fun too.

Why am I telling you this?

Because I often feel over-stretched, but I know that whenever my senses are dulled by fatigue the energy of the angels replenishes and fills me with a renewed sense of purpose and drive. Angels know that this passion for life and the spreading of encouragement to others fulfils my purpose and they help me all the time. I shall be on a mission to be the best that I can be, and to serve others and the planet as well as I am able, just like many of you.

The Divine needs a body. There is no coincidence that YOU are here now, doing your bit to change the world.

What will you do to bring Light into your own world? How will you shine your Light in service to others, to help to illuminate the bigger picture? I know that however "small" you consider yourself, or no matter how little you feel you are able to contribute, whatever you do it will be great. Even your loving smile brings lightness to the day. Know that you are SO loved by the Divine and the angelic realms.

Let us all shine from our hearts like beautiful stars, feeling happy, contented and fulfilled by the journey we are on. May the light of love glow on you and through you, and bless all those who come into contact with you.

REFERENCES

Introduction:
Step into Divine Light – Within and Without

1. The Essenes were the third largest religious sect during the time of Christ. It is believed that they lived in simple communities and practised the seventh day Sabbath, believed in reincarnation, non-violence to all living creatures and the sharing of all material possessions. Some were activists against Roman rule, but others were uninvolved in the politics of the Sadducees and Pharisees, and shunned town life by heading to the hillsides around Palestine, along the banks of the Dead Sea and the River Jordan. Within the Essenes were a group of ascetics who lived together in the mountains. Many were healers, and Jesus (Jeshua Ben Joseph) is believed to have been the one described as the "Teacher of Righteousness", referred to in the Dead Sea Scrolls.

2. www.greenmedinfo.com/blog/biophotons-human-body-emits-communicates-and-made-light; accessed 21 March 2017.

3. McTaggart, L. *The Field* (Element, 2003).

4. Theosophy means "God Wisdom", and is the study of any theological and philosophical ideas based on a direct experience of connection with the Divine. The term is used to describe any developed system of mystical thought and practice, such as the Kabbalah and Jakob Böhme.

Nowadays it is usually associated with the principles of the Theosophical Society, founded in 1875 by Madame Helena Petrovna Blavatsky and Henry Steel Olcott in New York, then in India and London. The Theosophical Society aimed to further the cause of world harmony by investigating the spiritual element of humanity and studying comparative religions, especially those in India. When Madame Blavatsky died, the work continued through Victorian reformist and suffragette Annie Besant. It became a catalyst in spreading ideas from the East to the West, particularly teachings from Buddhism and Hindu. Theosophical belief is that meditation is important, and Masters, first believed to come from Tibet, can guide that individual spiritual development. And that we will reincarnate many times, according to our deeds, and that the real aim of life is that we should achieve our real self (God self) aligning with the Divine will of the universal spirit. The Universe has seven planes, and we have seven bodies, each evolving towards a spiritual destiny. Although the society was heavily criticized for being "elitist", and Blavatsky was accused of being a fraud, Theosophical ideas have been a great influence on other religious movements, and in particular the New Age. One important member of the Theosophical Society – in terms of my work with angels – was Geoffrey Hodson, who was able to channel information about the angelic realms and record it in his beautiful book *The Brotherhood of Angels and Men*. He was guided and encouraged by an angelic being called Bethelda and his 1927 book is one of the earliest modern angel books available.

5. In Numerology, the study of the hidden significance of numbers, seven is sacred and holds the energy of the "ancient mystics". Someone whose personal birth or soul number is seven would be said to enjoy the mysterious side of life. A "seven" person is described as a seeker of truth and a thinker, who is likely to dedicate their lives to the search for deeper meaning. My own birth number is seven, which might help to explain why I am so intrigued by the magic and mystery of all things spiritual. So much so that I was called

to study world religions to degree level and spent many years understanding the Golden Thread of truth interweaving them all. (You can find your own birth number by adding all the numbers of your birthdate together: so, for example, if you were born, say, on 19 April 1964, the maths would be 1+9+4+1+9+6+4 = 34, 3+4 = 7.)

Tools for Your Journey:
How to Get the Best from This Book

1. Karma as an expression is entrenched within Hindu and Buddhist beliefs where all life is part of a constant wheel of birth–death–rebirth. Your deeds will follow through to the next lifetime. The word karma actually means "action" in Sanskrit. We have to take great care of our actions, as they will always have consequences. Nowadays it has come to mean "cause and effect" and we tend to use phrases such as "what goes around comes around" to describe someone's evil-doing in the hope that they will get their just desserts. In essence, the Law of Karma dictates that we pay the price of our actions. Whether good or bad, all our actions reflect back upon us, either in this life or in subsequent ones. Some cultures, in parts of Japan and Thailand for example, believe in "meritous" behaviour being stored up for future lifetimes, or for use of their future generations. I'm experiencing and noticing more "instant karma" in my life currently, where a good turn is instantly repaid.
2. www.nhs.uk/conditions/stress-anxiety-depression/pages/mindfulness.aspx; accessed 21 March 2017.
3. http://liveanddare.com/benefits-of-meditation/; accessed 21 March 2017.
4. Working with angels is different from the spirit guides drawn towards us in mediumship, or shamanism. The spirit guides, who may be of a very high vibration and may initiate channellings through you, if you have chosen to develop psychic abilities, have all been human beings and so have a different energy and vibration to that of angels. Nature spirits

and elemental energies which we may connect with through nature, or ritual, are a vital part of creation and may also have a strong connection with the angelic realms, but there are others who have more expertise in shamanic practices than I, so I have not included them here. Similarly, Ascended Masters may be mentioned as each of these seven Archangels works alongside a Mastered Being, but I don't intend to elaborate on the Ascended Masters here either. I will only be focusing on the angelic realms in this particular book.

5. This principle of manifestation, often referred to as the "Universal Law of Attraction", is now familiar to many of us. No one, of course, can say for certain how it works, but most of us would agree that we often see powerful evidence of this positive/negative energy exchange at work in our lives. Like light, sound too is a powerful energy form. In fact, every sound, whether it is an ocean wave, a dog bark or the human voice, carries its own vibration. When we utter our personal "sound", it is usually because we want to voice a thought, a need or an emotion. This in turn creates an energy force that manifests in our reality. So if the sound carries a positive charge, it gives a burst of brilliant energy to whatever we are intending to achieve and this is what we create. Similarly, if our thoughts contain a negative charge, which may also contain a strong negative emotion – such as resentment, bitterness, anger, etc. – this is "put out there" when expressed in aggressive language, giving power to that particular negative energy force. In other words, we can make things happen. It's what the ancients called "magic" and we now refer to as "intention".

6. A pure awareness and cosmic consciousness, also known as "enlightenment".

Step 1: Awaken to Your Soul Purpose

1. The space behind the forehead between the eyebrows is known as the "third eye" (also the brow or third eye chakra), and some Eastern cultures believe this is where the soul resides.

Step 2: Seek Your Inner Wisdom and Creativity

1. Archangel Jophiel is also known as Iofiel, Zophiel or Jofiel and means "Beauty of God".
2. This exercise was inspired by a learning exercise introduced to me by Mike King when I attended Surrey University.
3. This devotional practice is a fundamental part of all of the main religions where there is a belief in an actual personal God. The name we give to this comes from Hindu devotional practices and is called Bhakti. If you love God, these Divine beings and the angels, and use prayers, hymns or chanting in which you thank them, you have a sense of immense humility and gratitude.
4. www.bodysoulandspirit.net/mystical_experiences/read/notables/jung.shtml.
5. http://personalityspirituality.net/2010/07/23/the-swiss-mystic-and-his-big-red-book-the-secret-world-of-carl-g-jung/; accessed 13 May 2017.
6. Jung, C. *Jung on Synchronicity and the Paranormal* (Princeton University Press; Revised Edition, 1998).

Step 3: Practise Protection and Discernment

1. Archangel Michael's name means "He who is like God" in Hebrew.
2. An aura is a vibrating energy made up of our thoughts and patterns and is sometimes known as the etheric body. This energy body of light is as important as the physical light of our cells if we want optimum physical and mental health. A healthy aura contains strong colours and what can be described as an outer permeable "Light-body", and can be measured sometimes up to about 1.5m (5ft) around the body.

Step 4: Become Whole

1. www.sciencedaily.com/releases/2007/10/071009164122.htm; accessed 13 May 2017.

2. www.psychologytoday.com/conditions/post-traumatic-stress-disorder; accessed 13 May 2017.
3. www.psychologytoday.com/blog/urban-survival/201505/5-ways-stress-hurts-your-body-and-what-do-about-it; accessed 13 May 2017.

Step 5: Learn to Love

1. http://learn.genetics.utah.edu/content/epigenetics/rats/; accessed 13 May 2017.
2. www.health.harvard.edu/newsletter_article/the-health-benefits-of-strong-relationships; accessed 13 May 2017.
3. www.health.harvard.edu/healthbeat/the-power-of-self-compassion; accessed 13 May 2017.
4. www.psychologicalscience.org/observer/the-compassionate-mind#.WNpOehLyuV4; accessed 13 May 2017.
5. www.randomactsofkindness.org/kindness-research; accessed 13 May 2017.

Step 6: Transformation

1. www.sciencelearn.org.nz/resources/1304-positive-and-negative-effects-of-uv; accessed 13 May 2017.

APPENDIX

TABLE OF THE CHAKRAS

1. Root (or base) chakra – *Muladhara*

The root chakra carries all the qualities of our ancestors, and builds our support system. It sustains our stability, stamina and resilience, and our primary survival instinct. Opening the root chakra helps to ground us and trust in the goodness of life.

Location	At the base of the spine, coccyx, and in the perineum
Development	Conception to 7 years
Colour	Red
Crystals	Ruby, Carnelian, Bloodstone, Hematite
Archangels	Michael and Uriel
Endocrine connection	Connected to the cortex of the adrenal gland (on the outer edge of the kidneys), which is responsible for secretion of corticosteroids, cortisol and cortisone – steroid hormones. These trigger "fight or flight" reactions, which stimulate adrenaline to flow into our bloodstream so that we defend ourselves if we feel threatened.
Physical body	Feet, legs, hips, skeleton, kidneys, blood.
Problems (dysfunction)	Fatigue, arthritis, kidney stones, osteoporosis, autoimmune diseases and bone deficiencies. Low energy and life force, disempowerment, dependency on others, "victimhood".
Life lessons	To learn trust, self-sufficiency, perseverance, patience, structure and the ability to notice the perfection and beauty in nature, feel secure and manifest your dreams.
Affirmation	"I trust that I am creating a secure, supportive structure in my life that is wholesome and good."

2. Sacral chakra – *Swvatistana*

The sacral chakra supports our sense of wellbeing and capacity to enjoy life and all its physical pleasures. Connected to our feelings it governs our emotions, sensuality and sexuality and its function depends on how much we feel we are deserving of the good things in life, receiving pleasure, joy, abundance and good health.

Location	Centre of the pelvis, lower abdomen, between the pubic bone and the navel
Development	7–14 years
Colour	Orange
Crystals	Tiger's Eye, Carnelian
Archangels	Gabriel and Jophiel
Endocrine connection	Ovaries in women, testes in men, which control sexual development and reproduction.
Physical body	Sex organs, bladder, uterus in women, prostate in men.
Problems (dysfunction)	Creates all sensuality issues, eating disorders and gynaecological problems in women such as menstrual cramps, endometriosis, inability to conceive, fibroids and cystitis. In men it can cause infertility, sexual dysfunction, sciatica and prostate problems.
Life lessons	This energy helps us to develop sexual health and fulfilment, ease with change, fluidity, creativity, grace, balanced emotions and healthy boundaries and a healthy acceptance of the physical world and its abundant pleasures.
Affirmation	"I love and respect myself, honouring my body, affirming my worth as the beauty and joy of life resonates with my soul."

3. Solar plexus chakra – *Manipura*

The solar plexus chakra helps us to process what we take in and is vital for the digestion of both food and ideas. It is directly related to the ego, and the quality of our relationships with others and the wider world. It is also involved with our sense of self-value, personal power and passion for life. It encourages leadership whilst appreciating solitude.

Location	Under the sternum, over the stomach
Development	14–21 years
Colour	Yellow
Crystals	Citrine, Amber, Topaz
Archangels	Michael and Jophiel
Endocrine connection	Pancreas, which processes sugars and controls the digestion of food, releasing energy into the system.
Physical body	Stomach, liver, spleen, pancreas, small intestine, muscles.
Problems (dysfunction)	Diabetes, indigestion, constipation, stomach ulcers, hyper-acidity, gallstones, pancreatitis, and hepatitis.
Life lessons	Developing a strong and balanced ego, personal power, will, effectiveness, personal energy.
Affirmation	"I am confident in my choices, accepting the power of my Light and love, knowing that I am a powerful force for good."

4. Heart chakra – *Anahata*

The heart energy seeks love in every situation and blossoms when the energy of pure love is allowed to expand. The qualities of the heart chakra are peace, purity, love, joy and unity.

Location	Centre of the body, in the middle of the chest
Development	21–28 years
Colour	Green and pink
Crystals	Rose quartz, Peridot, Emerald, Diamond
Archangels	Raphael and Chamuel
Endocrine connection	Thymus gland
Physical body	Heart, lungs, pericardium and circulation.
Problems (dysfunction)	Heart and lung disease, such as angina, arteriosclerosis, myocardial infarction (heart attack) and arrhythmia. Lung diseases include breathing disorders, tuberculosis, bronchitis, pneumonia, asthma and minor chest infections.
Life lessons	Ability to feel compassion, learn to love deeply without conditions; forgiveness, develop healthy intimate relationships, and acceptance and love of self.
Affirmation	"My core is pure and I anchor my heart in warmth, truth, love and the Divine's grace as I radiate joy in the world."

5. Throat chakra – *Visuddha*

The throat chakra is known as the gateway to the higher spiritual planes. At the base of the brain, the medulla oblongata is said to be the area where higher spiritual energy is channelled into the body. To keep this energy centre healthy we must develop a strong sense of truth and personal integrity. It is our centre of communication and will. Suppressed emotions and unexpressed ideas will block this chakra.

Location	External and internal throat and neck, mouth and jaw
Development	28–35 years
Colour	Sky blue/turquoise
Crystals	Turquoise, Aquamarine, Blue Agate, Blue Topaz
Archangel	Gabriel
Endocrine connection	Thyroid gland controls metabolism and assists growth and affects development both physically and mentally.
Physical body	Heart, lungs, pericardium and circulation.
Problems (dysfunction)	Laryngitis and sore throat, deafness, teeth decay, gum disease and cervical neck problems.
Life lessons	Learning about truthful relationships. The right to speak. Learning to express yourself and your beliefs (truthful expression). Ability to trust. Loyalty. Organization and planning. Clear communication. Develop the ability to express one's self, manifest personal essence in the world, and a rich creative life.
Affirmation	"I keep my word, live in my integrity and communicate my truth clearly at all times."

6. Brow (third eye) chakra – *Anja*

Known as the "control" centre, the brow chakra focuses on cultivating a strong and intelligent mind. Brown chakra energy stimulates both sides of the brain, enables us to develop clear and concise thoughts, ideas, wisdom and discernment, intuition and spiritual understanding.

Location	In the middle of the forehead just above the brow line
Development	35–42 years
Colour	Indigo
Crystals	Lapis Lazuli, Sapphire, Tanzanite
Archangels	Michael and Jophiel
Endocrine connection	Pituitary gland is the controlling gland for other hormones including growth and those produced during childbirth and also influences our metabolism.
Physical body	Eyes, sinuses, base of skull and temporal lobes.
Problems (dysfunction)	Intelligence or learning problems, migraine, cataracts, glaucoma and blindness, strokes and brain tumours.
Life lessons	Developing intuition or the right to "see". Trusting your intuition and insights. Developing psychic abilities. Self-realization. Releasing hidden and repressed negative thoughts.
Affirmation	"As I tap into my inner wisdom I am open to the Light in my world."

7. Crown chakra– *Sahasrara*

The crown chakra connects us to the cosmos, to our divinity, and is the source of heightened spiritual development, of Christ consciousness. It is the centre where, when open, we experience a relationship with the Divine.

Location	Top of and above the head
Development	42 years onwards
Colour	Violet
Crystal	Amethyst
Archangels	Zadkiel
Endocrine connection	Pineal gland, which regulates our body clock by producing melatonin.
Physical body	Top of the skull, brain (cerebral cortex) and skin.
Problems (dysfunction)	Problems with learning, perception, comprehension and spiritual development as well as colour blindness, neurosis, depression, anxiety, alcoholism, insomnia and epilepsy.
Life lessons	Knowingness and the right to aspire. Dedication to the Divine and universal consciousness; trusting the Universe. Learning about our spirituality: our connection to the concept of "God", the Divine or a higher intelligence. Integrating your consciousness and sub-consciousness into the "one-ness" with understanding.
Affirmation	"I live in gratitude and joy, accepting who I am and the Divine spirit within me."

ABOUT THE AUTHOR

Chrissie Astell is one of the UK's best-loved spiritual educators and angel experts. Having worked as a registered nurse specialising in the care of the elderly and dying, Chrissie has had direct experience of the profound effect of the loving and healing energy of angels. Her 1997 vision of "an angel carrying a heart" led her to dedicate her life to helping people to connect with their own guardian angels.

Chrissie's intuitive gifts are supported by extensive academic study. She holds a BA Hons in Comparative Religion (SOAS), along with postgraduate certificates in Development and Facilitation, and Adult Education. Her teachings have brought thousands of people into closer relationship with angelic guardians, healing energies and universal love.

As well as the workshops she offers throughout the UK, Chrissie runs courses in Spiritual Development and Facilitation, including a Diploma programme for people who wish to develop skills to teach and facilitate spiritual growth in others. She has also created a unique and comprehensive home-study course, *Educating Heart and Soul*. She has written a number of books, including *Gifts from Angels*, *Discovering Angels*, *Advice from Angels* and *The Guardian Angel Oracle*, a deck of 52 illustrated oracle cards with accompanying guide.

Chrissie regularly features as an angel expert on the radio and television, and has written features for a range of press, including *Kindred Spirit*, *Watkins Review* and *The Telegraph*.

For further information, check out AngelLight.co.uk and ChrissieAstell.com.